All my best

[signature]

THE GOD BIT

Joey Adams

THE
GOD BIT

Mason & Lipscomb PUBLISHERS   NEW YORK

ISBN: 0–88405–086–6
Library of Congress Catalog Card Number: 74–5430

Printed in the United States of America

First Printing

Grateful acknowledgment is made for permission to quote from the following:

"A New Song," by Pat Boone. © 1973 by Creation House. Reprinted by permission.

From *The Raw Pearl* and *Talking to Myself*, by Pearl Bailey. Reprinted by permission of Harcourt, Brace, Jovanovich, Inc.

From the poem "I Cannot Grieve . . ." by June Lockhart. Reprinted by permission of *Guideposts*.

From *Yes I Can* by Sammy Davis, Jr., Jane and Burt Boyar, copyright © 1965 by Sammy Davis, Jr., Jane Boyar and Burt Boyar. Reprinted with the permission of Farrar, Straus & Giroux, Inc.

Bob Considine's columns, "A Newspaperman's Prayer" and "Dear Jesus" are reprinted by permission of King Features Syndicate.

From "Can Archie Bunker Be Saved," from *St. Anthony Messenger*.

From *De Mille* by Charles Higham, reprinted with permission of Charles Scribner's Sons.

From Sammy Cahn's "Look to Your Heart," © 1955 Barton Music Corp., New York City.

From "We Shall Overcome," new words and new music arr. by Zilphia Horton, Frank Hamilton, Guy Carawan and Pete Seeger. TRO—© copyright 1960 & 1963 Ludlow Music, Inc., New York, N.Y. Used by permission.

Library of Congress Cataloging in Publication Data

Adams, Joey, 1911–
  The God bit.

  1. Entertainers—Religious life. I. Title.
BV4596.E67A3   248'.4   74–5430
ISBN 0–88405–086–6

To my Co-Author
"For He performeth the thing
that is appointed for me."
Job 23:14

Contents

Preface

Show people are the first to announce their beliefs in God and themselves—and I know in this case they'll forgive me for giving God top billing.

Most people in show business live by the old switch bit, "Don't keep the faith—spread it around." The fact is, the God Bit has always been a headliner in the theater. There are no atheists in the dressing rooms.

I know one actor who wrote a book about atheism—and then prayed it would be a best seller. I really feel sorry for the poor atheist who is doing good and feels grateful—but has nobody to thank.

Any fool can prove that the Bible ain't so—it takes a wise man to believe it.

You learn soon enough in show business that you can't do it out there alone—God is your co-star. Even a card-carrying nonbeliever who wouldn't be caught in church—even on a bingo night—is going to look for a little help from the manager in the sky when he's going on opening night. It's New Haven, the first act is weak, the audience is light, it's raining—at the very least he'll say, "Please, God, make the critics be in a good mood."

Or, if he sees a skinny little chorus girl rubbing her rabbit's foot or saying her beads, he'll say, "Put in a good word for me." At the very worst, it can't hurt.

One actor I know offered a special prayer before opening night: "Please God, help me make a big hit tonight. You help little nobody actors, civilians, complete strangers, even chorus girls—Why not help me—a star?"

Ginger Rogers told me she never goes onstage without thinking, "Man is not a worker, he is God's work going on." Ginger always remembers what Sir Harry Lauder told her when she was a little girl. She asked the great variety star if he ever got butterflies before he went onstage—if he was nervous, afraid. "No," he answered, "I close my eyes and realize love is out there—I love them and they love me!"

Jane Russell says, "God is a living doll. I was put on this earth to glorify Him. How can I lose if I let Him do it for me?"

In show business, that kind of talk is called doing the God bit. Everything in show business is a "bit" or a "thing" or a *shtick*. Doing the God bit means doing your thing with the Lord or getting on the Faith kick—each in his own way.

And I'm sure God doesn't mind our language. If Jesus came to town today he wouldn't talk about shepherds or publicans but about riots and law and order and revolution—and in a language we would all understand.

Prayer is love. It's not important to say "beseech" when you mean "ask" or "thy" when you mean "you." If it comes easier for you to say "I'll do it your way," instead of "thy will be done," you can bet that the God who is love will dig it. I keep laughing at Bert Wheeler's great line in his vaudeville act when he said, "Don't worry—the man is coming with the quilt," and his partner replied, "You mean the comforter cometh."

Not everybody who accepts an Infinite Power who has created the heavens and the earth "and created man upon it" is of the Bible-thumping, psalm-singing variety. Some of them are baldly irreverent about Him. Some others haven't been in a church or synagogue or come-as-you-are mosque since the day they had those baptismal drops sprinkled on them.

x

Nonetheless, even though they don't approach with their hands clasped in prayer position, they know He's there when they need Him.

One such fella is Frank Sinatra, who told me, "First I believe in you and me. I'm like Albert Schweitzer, Bertrand Russell and Albert Einstein in that I have a respect for life in any form. I believe in nature, in the birds, in the sky, in everything I can see or there is real evidence for. If these things are what you mean by God, then I believe in God.

"But I don't believe in a personal God to whom I look for comfort or for a natural on the next roll of the dice.

"I'm not unmindful of man's seeming need for faith; I'm for anything that gets you through the night—be it prayer, tranquilizers or a bottle of Jack Daniels.

"But to me, religion is a deeply personal thing in which man and God go it alone together, without the witch doctor in the middle who tries to convince us that we have to ask God for help, to spell out to Him what we need, even to bribe Him with prayer or cash on the line.

"Well, I believe that God knows what each of us wants and needs. It is not necessary for us to make it to church on Sunday to reach Him. You can find Him anyplace—and if that sounds heretical, my source is pretty good: Matthew, Five to Seven, the Sermon on the Mount."

Georgie Jessel says, "Belief in God is good whether you practice it in a church, a synagogue or a shrine. If such a building is too far away, call your mother. If she is not within reach, tell it to the trees, or better still, buy a meal for a fellow that's hungry and a drink, too, if you can afford it. If you're broke, call me up and I'll buy you both the meal, the drink and a cigar, too. But hurry up, do it while I'm still around."

Each of us does the God bit in our own way. God knows no two of us is alike. After all, He is the big Producer that's putting on this whole show and he is far more original and creative than the most artistic person on earth. He didn't waste his time making carbons of people.

Helen Hayes, the first lady of the theater, is one of God's great, special creations. "As we grow older," Miss Hayes told me, "God sees to it our eyesight grows dimmer, so that when we look at ourselves in the mirror we can say, 'I still look as good as ever.'"

It was Will Rogers who said, "The minute a thing is long and complicated it confuses. Whoever wrote the Ten Commandments made them short. They may not always be kept, but they are understood. They are the same for all men.

"Moses went up the mountain with a letter of credit and some instructions from the Lord and he just wrote them out and they applied to the oil men, the steel men, the farmer, the bankers and even the U.S. Chamber of Commerce.

"I expect there are a lot of lessons in the Bible that we could learn and profit by and help us out, but we are just so busy doing nothing we haven't got time to study them out. But in Moses' time the rich didn't gang up on you and say 'You change that commandment or we won't play.'

"You can't get far ridiculing a man for upholding the Bible or even the dictionary—if it's his sincere belief."

Some of the greatest one-liners in history outside of the Ten Commandments and Milton Berle will never be found in the Bible. Baseball star Bobby Richardson offered the shortest prayer of all: "Dear God, your will, nothing more, nothing less, nothing else—Amen!"

Remember when Champ Joe Louis faced a war-weary audience at Madison Square Garden and said, "We cannot lose —God is on our side."

It was my dear friend Martin Luther King, Jr., who said, "I will love the hell out of you."

Mickey Rooney says that people often mistake him for John Wayne: "His eye patch and me are the same size." He claims that he is a blessed man having been allowed to make so many mistakes in his marriages and divorces. He explains his return to God and the church and says, "Life has been nice as I stumble through the Ten Commandments."

Like my pal Bob Hope says: "I know that religion is coming back—Dial-A-Prayer just ordered three more numbers."

Show people are the greatest salesmen for the God bit. It's not true that the Lord and the people He created to glorify

Him do not want to get involved. If the stars can come out for their favorite candidate, they certainly can come out for the Superstar. If show people can endorse cigarettes and razor blades, they sure can endorse the Almighty. Don't the kids eat a breakfast cereal because Joe Namath eats it? Won't they use a toothpaste that Billie Jean King uses? Won't the fans want to sit in the same pew with their idols?

Faith is a star and each terrestrial star has his own philosophy. Tom Jones claims he lives each day as though it's his last day on earth. When I told this to eighty-nine-year-old Harry Hershfield, he said, "I live each day as though it's my first day on earth."

Each of us does the God bit in his own way. Like the actor's little girl who received a paint set for Christmas. The seven-year-old was working hard to make a picture when her father came home and asked what it was she was painting.

"It's a picture of God."

"Darling," he said, "that's very sweet, but nobody ever saw God. Nobody knows what he looks like."

"Well," she said, "*now* they'll know."

To find God you must seek Him. You must work at it. Just as the squirrel stores up nuts for the winter and the comic salts away the heckle lines until he needs them, so must we do the same with faith and love. Those golden thoughts come in handy should we ever be in need.

Did you hear the story about the agent who hated actors? His biggest pleasure was telling some unemployed actor: "Don't call us—we'll call you!" When television came along and there were no theaters for him to book, he suddenly discovered God and begged for help. The legend goes that God sent an angel down to see him. The angel listened to his lament, then said, "Don't call us—we'll call you!"

I learned that lesson from Billy Rose. The famed producer, songwriter and millionaire was reading the proofs of my first book, *From Gags to Riches,* and thought I should delete some of the stories that might hurt people, especially the ones about him, even if it was meant only in jest. "Read it all over carefully," he suggested, "before you go to press. . . . It will keep you from walking into lamp posts later in life."

It's all there in the story of the little boy who was scrubbed by his mom, dressed in spotless linen and put out into the yard with the warning, "Don't play with anyone. We're going to visit Grandma and I want you to look nice." But another kid called him a sissy and they were soon rolling in the dirt. After the tussle was over, an ice-cream cart passed and the bedraggled moppet ran into the house to get a dime. His mom took one look at him and remarked, "Are you in a position to ask for favors?"

Walt Frazier, the great Knicks basketball star, says, "Everybody goes to God when they are doing bad. I go to Him when I'm doing good. When I don't need Him is when I thank Him the most."

That's the faith that moves mountains as well as audiences, producers and even critics—when you believe, even if you're not in need.

That's the kind of faith kids have. My five-year-old niece slipped into bed without saying her prayers one night, explaining to her mother, "There are some nights when I don't want anything."

Shirley Booth says : "I've not always been a dutiful Christian, but I've always been a believing Christian."

The star of "Hazel" on TV and the lady who received an Oscar for *Come Back, Little Sheba* and a Tony for *Time of the Cuckoo* used to sing in the choir in the Episcopal church. "For a time, I was very much in rebellion," Shirley says, "because I had to go to church three times on Sunday. And I think children get fed up a little bit and it takes a little while for them to come back to the fold. But I'm back now and loving it."

Miss Booth's philosophy of life is told in a poem that she found and that she says she lives by:

> Give me a good digestion, Lord, and also something to
> digest.
> Give me a healthy body, Lord, and the sense to keep it
> at its best.

Give me a healthy mind, Lord, and keep the good and
   pure in sight.
When seeing sin be not appalled, but find a way to
   set it right.
Give me a mind that is not bored, that does not whimper,
   whine or sigh.
Don't let me worry overmuch about this fussy thing
   called I.
Give me a sense of You, My Lord, give me the grace to
   see a joke.
To find some happiness in life and pass it on to other
   folks.

That's the idea of this book. Not to keep the faith, but to spread
it around.

I love show people for their illusions, just as much as I love
them for their talents, their exaggerations, their persistence,
their guts and their faith and belief in God and themselves. I
love the kind of humor that runs in their funny bones. I don't
know who said it—I think it was me—"Show people are a chip
off God's funnybone." They have an odd, a philosophical, a
wonderful, an exclusive kind of humor that proves with every
studied ad-lib that there's no business like show business and
no people like show people.

I guess show people do more benefits than anybody and
thus, they're able to store up love, faith and joy for that rainy
day and that goes for tons of singers, dancers, musicians and
performers of every shape, size and talent who are in there
doing the God bit. That's why I'm putting down their story—
so that some of it could rub off on all of us.

It's the story of Kathryn Crosby, the actress-wife of Bing,
who lives by a saying told to her by her mother, "Living,
Kathy, is giving."

It's the story of Muhammad Ali, who credits his broken
jaw at the hands of Ken Norton with "not being prayed up."
He claims he was "spiritually unfit and was sinning too much."
He meant it, too, and claims he learned a lot.

I want to tell you about Dennis Day, who has a slogan and an attitude that is just beautiful. His slogan is, "Yes, please." It's an attitude of being ready to respond to requests of others. He believes people who say "No," or "No, thanks," are looking down. But a "Yes, please," attitude means looking up—being confident—in oneself, in one's fellow men, in God.

Ethel Waters says that she bared herself to God late in life and he crumbled her and put her back together again His way —the way she was meant to be in the first place.

"I don't get lonely no more," Ethel says now, "because God is with me—but I do understand the person who *is* lonely. A long time ago when I had so much of what the world counts necessary, I was so lonely. Now that I have so little of that, loneliness is out—because I have so much to be thankful for and when you're thankful, you can't be lonely—or sorry for yourself."

You'll hear a lot about my friend Pat Boone who is "fighting to help a sick world—families are disintegrating, people are crying out, searching for answers—they're turning to drugs, sex, rebellion and even satanic worship and witchcraft.

"I can just hear God looking down and saying, '*Now* are you ready to listen to Me?'"

Pat says, "Most of the excitement in our lives came from discovering that the Bible is as current and immediate as today's newspaper—and a lot more accurate. It should be; it was programmed by the same heavenly computer that hung the stars."

I can't wait to tell you the stories of Jerry Lewis and Jackie Gleason, of Sammy Davis, Jr. and Alan Young, of Johnny Cash and Lionel Hampton.

Lionel Hampton, the all-time jazz great, uses the Bible for healing. "We never used medicine in my home," Lionel told me. "Once I was supposed to be operated on for appendicitis. My grandmother healed me with the Bible and I've been on it ever since.

"Years later a doctor looked at me and said, 'You had a beautiful operation. You can't see the scar. Who did it?' I just laughed and said, 'I don't know,' but to myself I said, 'Dr. Jesus.' "

Even the little actors have a story. Did I tell you the one about the unemployed hoofer who came home singing and dancing, filled with joy and his wife asked, "Why are you so happy? You know we have nothing in the house." He answered, "I know we have nothing to eat—but thank God I have a good appetite."

Jackie Gleason was born a Catholic. "I'm still a Catholic," the great one says. "The reason is that I am also a sinner. I'm not too good of a Catholic, but when you're a sinner it's very nice to know when you're sinning.

"Because it hurts a little more and that's what religion is. It's not supposed to be all gravy. It's not supposed to be something that makes you jump up and shout 'Hallelulah.' It's supposed to hurt you. It's supposed to stick you with a pin and every time you do something wrong and you get stuck with that pin, you think it over and if you want to get stuck with that pin again and it's worth it—then you sin again."

That's the big reason that Jackie refused to join Billy Graham when he was asked to go on tour with him. "I believe," he explained, "but the life I've led, I don't think I'd be a good ad for the Man Upstairs."

Johnny Cash has a great story to tell. Through the power of prayer, Johnny overcame his past, his prison record, his drinking, his fight against drugs. He fought and he prayed his way to stardom and the idol of millions.

Johnny has used his new-found fame and money to build a church in his hometown—a monument to God in appreciation for His help in guiding him through the bad times and leading him to a better, fuller life.

You will never meet a nicer man than Jack Benny. "God doesn't lay out your life," Jack says. "Does he lay out wars? Sickness? Accidents? Of course not. He only lays out good—but you have to accept it and make your own life. You've got to do your own thing. Nobody can do it for you. You've got to make your own deals."

That's what my friend Bishop Fulton Sheen told the State Legislature of New York when he addressed them. "I'm not going to pray for you. There are certain things a man has to do for himself. He has to blow his own nose, make his own love, and say his own prayers."

In this book you will find stories of many of the stars you have always believed in. Now you will get a chance to find out how they believe.

Mostly we will talk about love. And when you talk about love it must rub off on somebody around you sooner or later. My beautiful Cindy has a habit of pasting her favorite sayings on the refrigerator, the night table, her desk or the bathroom mirror—great one-liners like: "God is love," or "Thinking good is thanking God," or "You shall know the truth and the truth shall set you free."

They were all just phrases to me. Nice. But like a Milton Berle punchline, it's good—but where can I use it? Until one bad day in Indonesia, Cindy and I were driving from Bandung to Djakarta in about 105° heat and her fever was higher. She was too sick to work for herself or sing her favorite hymns, which always helped her before.

How I wished I knew those phrases now that were pasted all over our house. I prayed for help. "I don't know the words," I said, "but I need Your help so much."

Suddenly the words from the Bible jumped up at me: "And a little child shall lead them." I remembered, "God's arms are above, below and around you all the time." I remembered, "Wherever I am—God is—and if that be true there is no safer, healthier, happier place to be than where I am," and "God is all—and God is good." So wherever we are God is and that means good is.

It all gushed out—all the one-liners that were just punchlines—now had a meaning: "Trust in the Lord with all thy heart and lean not unto thy own understanding. In all thy ways acknowledge Him. And He will direct thy path."

We started singing hymns—to this day I don't know how I remembered the words—and by the time we reached Djakarta, my Cindy was well.

xviii

You are too, if you want to let Him in. Try it, you'll like it. Come on in and have your faith lifted.

At each entrance to the Pentagon in Washington is a large sign for all to read: "Worship daily according to your faith." Whether or not those who read it heed this good advice is, in America, still a matter for them alone to decide. At the very least, this book will give you a chance to make up your own mind.

However, I just wanted to point out that there is no such sign at the entrance of the Kremlin. You will find none in Peking. There was none at the door to Hitler's Reich Chancellory.

Chapter 1.

Faith Is a Star

Faith is a star. That goes for everybody, whether you're on-stage or sitting in the balcony. No matter how high you are soaring or how far down, you can reach God. He's waiting for you, waiting to prove his love for you. All you need is faith—faith in God as our Father and men as our brothers.

Billing isn't too important to the Big Producer in the sky. He doesn't have a part you must fit—He's good to the entire cast. Anybody who wants a part in His show is welcome. He has no favorites. Everybody is His special star. With Him, we're all stars.

As the sun shines on all of us, so does the light of God pour down on rich men, poor men, beggar men, thieves, doctors, lawyers, comedians and even New York taxicab drivers. In like measure does that hydra-headed, swollen dragon called Evil or Satan or Problem try to heckle us no matter who or where we are.

But if we believe, God has the squelches.

If you don't believe me, let me quote from the best seller of all time—it's even outsold Jacqueline Susann or Mickey Spillane—it's called the Bible:

3

"Come unto me ye that labour and are heavy laden, and I will give you rest." (Matthew 11:28)

"Cast thy burden upon the Lord and He will sustain you." (Psalms 55:22)

"Lo, I am with you always, even unto the end of the world." (Matthew 28:20)

"Be not afraid, neither be thou dismayed. For the Lord thy God is with thee whithersoever thou goest." (Joshua 1:9)

All right, now do you believe me? Sure, go to God when you're doing badly—but don't forget to tell Him when you're doing well, too.

Jane Russell reminded me of all this when we were playing the RKO in Boston. I was down because some friends had proved ungrateful. "Don't look for good to come back to you," Jane scolded. "Look for it to do good to those you help. You can't bargain with God."

"I know," I said, "but I helped this bum when he was nothing and now he's going around town telling people that I'm suffering from 'I' strain—that I'm so conceited, I have to have my X-rays retouched. I can't understand all this talk. I insist I'm not conceited—although I have every right to be."

"Oh," said Jane, "the Lord loves the humble spirit. He says, 'Humble thyself, and I will exalt thee.' Isn't that a comforting thing? *Humble thyself. You* have to do the humbling—*He* does the exalting. So, I want to tell you something. If you don't humble yourself, He knows how to do it! And you'll never forget it!"

That's how I got my first Bible. The star of *The Outlaw* gave it to me backstage at the RKO Boston and she quoted reassuringly in the dedication to me: "All things work together for good for those who love the Lord." She signed it *Old Jane*.

"Old Jane" sure needed some of that faith she had been spreading around when she was in trouble recently. It's a good thing she kept some of it for herself—even though it was lying dormant for awhile.

"I was in a pit," Jane told me, "because my husband had died and I was not up to uplifting anyone—especially myself.

4

I was practically out of show business and ready to pack it all in when I was offered the lead in *Company* on Broadway. It was a perfect part for me and ordinarily I would have jumped at it, but I wasn't in tune with the Big Man. I gave myself all kinds of excuses: 'Only two and a half weeks to rehearse . . . The Sondheim music is too difficult . . . I don't want to make a fool of myself.' The jitters really set in. I was panicky.

"The Lord finally backed me into a corner, where I could let the frenzy pass and think. I found a little book by Norman Vincent Peale, which I read from cover to cover and came away with:

" 'This is the day the Lord hath made—let us rejoice and be glad in it.'

" 'I sought the Lord, and he answered me and delivered me from all my fears.

" 'Try, really try, think, really think, believe, really believe.

" 'Drop all your problems into a pool of quietness—in quietness and trust shall be my strength.'

"It was as though the Lord said, 'I've opened doors all your life. You've been obedient before, so why balk now? If I open doors no man can close, should you be afraid? Others would give their souls for such a chance and you're running away. If I open the door, I give you the ability to go through it. Trust me!' "

Well, the rest is history. "Old Jane" came back bigger and better than ever. "Faith sure is a star," she told me. "The wheel has turned again and life, once more, is great."

That's the whole idea. You've got to stand still and listen for God. If you want the Almighty, all you have to do is accept Him, instead of accepting Evil.

It brings to mind the routine Buck and Bubbles, the great vaudeville stars, used to do:

BUBBLES: Where were you running in such a hurry when I saw you this afternoon?

BUCK: It was lightning and I was running to a cellar to hide.

BUBBLES: Are you crazy? Don't you know if lightning is gonna get you—it's gonna get you!

BUCK: If lightning is gonna get me, let him look for me.

It's the same thing with Evil. If you run to God, old Beelzebub, the Devil's agent, can look for you all day—he'll never be able to get you.

That's the story of Johnny Cash. His records sold in the millions. His starring on the Grand Old Opry and personal appearances brought the world to his feet—but he threw it all away on drugs.

"I thought I needed those pills to stay alive. I took pep pills to turn me on and depressants to calm me down. Then I began to realize that the highs were getting lower and the few pills a day weren't enough. I had to go from a few to several, then to dozens. I was always nervous and tense and irritable. I didn't want to eat. I couldn't sleep. I started losing weight.

"I knew I was killing myself. I had seen drugs kill others. Whatever drug an addict is hooked on, he has to keep increasing his daily dosage. The day comes when he takes the overdose that kills him. Knowing this, I accepted early death as the inescapable fate of addicts. There was no other way out. Even when I thought of all the things I had to be thankful for, I could find no hope for myself, no chance for change."

What a shock to the world when Cash was first arrested on a drug charge. The judge let him off with a year's suspended sentence, but that didn't change Johnny until one day he crossed the Georgia border and found himself staring at a ceiling, with an elderly jailer asking him if he felt better.

"I found you in a daze wandering around town, so I brought you here," the officer said. "I didn't want you to hurt yourself."

"How much time do you think I'll get for this?" Cash asked.

"You're doing time right now, Johnny, the worst kind," he answered. He handed him an envelope. "Here are your things.

6

I'm a fan of yours, Johnny. I've always admired you. It's a shame to see you ruining yourself. I didn't know you were this bad off."

Johnny had heard this song before. "Okay, sure," he said.

The officer couldn't be nicer. "I don't know where you think you got your talent from," he said, "but if you think it came from God, then you're sure wrecking the body He put it in."

"Sure—thanks," Johnny said. "Can I go now?"

"That morning, as I stepped into the morning sunshine," Johnny said later, "I took a quick but deep look at my life over the past seven years—and knew that I was a better man than that.

"Maybe it was the reference to God that suddenly cleared my mind. My parents were religious, all right. Faith had always meant a lot to me. But until that morning it hadn't occurred to me to turn to God for help in kicking my habit.

"Suddenly I remembered: God had given me a free will and like a fool I decided to experiment with the drugs that had now robbed me of it. I realized that to be free again I would need all the will power I could acquire and I knew this power could only come from God, who had created me free. I asked Him to work on me then and there."

When he got back to Nashville he told his friends, "I'm kicking the habit as of now. I don't expect it will be easy, so I'll need your help. See to it that I eat regular meals, and that I keep regular hours. If I can't sleep, sit and talk to me. If we run out of talk, let's pray.

"We sure prayed a lot. I am a free man now, as I have been since that morning when I discovered that I could be once again.

"Because I'm in show business, it's pretty difficult to sweep past mistakes under the rug. Every so often, I meet some kid who knows I used to be an addict, as he is now, and he asks me what he can do to kick the habit. I tell him what I learned: 'Give God's temple back to Him. The alternative is death.'"

Faith sure is a star, and each star makes it in his own way. The Presbyterian church in Bel Air, California is jumping because Marge Champion got hooked on God. You can find her in church almost every week, dancing for the Sunday evening service—and there's music, folk and rock, banners, balloons—and everyone there dancing and lifting their voices in joyous prayer.

"We have forgotten that God knows how to laugh," Marge explains. "We shouldn't be ashamed to show our emotions when we worship Him."

It all began a few years before when the pastor of the church asked Marge and Steve Allen and several other show-business folks, what wasn't happening in churches that wasn't reaching people.

All they had to offer was their talents, like the juggler of Notre Dame, who gave the Christ child the only gift he had—his juggling. The pastor accepted, and the show went on. They call it "creative worship," and the church swings with everything from Yemenite dancers performing a 2500-year-old Hebrew wedding dance to the choreography of the Lord's Prayer.

Marge Champion produces these programs now for quite a few churches, and she never looked better or felt better. She's fifty-five now, and is as lovely and lithe as she was when she teamed with her former husband Gower Champion in theaters, clubs and pictures in the 1950s.

For Marge, faith is stardom. "At one time I thought I had everything," Marge says now. "I was a star on the stage, I was married to Gower, I had two sons, I enjoyed my friends and my home, but there was a hole in my life and I didn't know what it was.

"One day I went to a religious service and cried through the whole thing. I couldn't explain why. Maybe God was trying to tell me something—but what?

"Then I got a phone call from a good friend who was really hurting. The friend was Debbie Reynolds. Eddie Fisher, her husband then, was tangled with Elizabeth Taylor. Debbie asked me to go to church with her. If she had asked me to go to a ball game I would have. Anyway, I went and I continued to go, mostly as an observer.

8

"One day the minister asked me, 'When will you really be part of this?'

" 'I don't know if I can say the words,' I said.

" 'All it takes to begin with,' the minister said, 'is a grain of faith no bigger than a mustard seed. Do you have that much?'

"I had at least that much," Marge said, "and I got hooked."

She sure needed it when her twenty-five-year marriage blew up—but it flowered when she brought the magic of her dancing into church and proved that there are more ways to worship God than this world dreams of.

Pat O'Brien is another star who says, "Faith is my life." The star of one hundred motion pictures or more, admits now that, "My world may not be as wide as Einstein's, as deep as sunk in secret darkness as Freud's, as wild and cruel as Marx's, but my world is inhabited by the great shadows of Moses and Abraham, the teachings of Isaiah and Jeremiah and the eternal words of the divinity of Jesus Christ.

"The prayer of faith I learned at my mother's knee set the standard of living and of loving ever since, and I would not surrender it for all the rewards in the world."

Kate Smith is one of the all-time superstars. She's been in the Big Time for almost fifty years and she's loaded. In fact, she could have retired twenty-five years ago.

Ask the "God Bless America" lady why she didn't, and she says, "Because God gave me this musical ability to use, and like fine wine, it gets better. Talent which comes from God must be appreciated.

"I know my voice is a Divine gift because I didn't utter a word until I was four. My mother thought I was a deaf-mute. Then one day she heard what she thought was a neighbor's child singing and she called, 'Is that you, Kathryn?' I replied, 'Yes, mother,' and those were the first words I spoke. From then on I haven't stopped."

Kate believes the reason she didn't speak until then was that the Lord was developing her vocal chords. "And now that

9

He's developed them, I intend to keep right on using 'em."

"How come you never married?" I asked the sixty-five-year-old Kate Smith.

"I've had many opportunities," she explained, "but I'm a perfectionist. I decided I couldn't give my all to a husband and a career, so I chose the career. That's another reason I'll never stop singing. I've given too much else to it."

"I know," I said, "but aren't you ever lonely?"

"Lonely?" she said. "I'm never alone. Remember, I believe in God and I know He's always with me. How could I be lonely?"

There is a point in each person's life when he has nowhere to go but up. Helen Hayes reached that point in 1949 when her only daughter, Mary, died of polio. But that real gut question —Why?—was unanswered. Mary was young and beautiful. Why? Why? Why?

Helen Hayes began to search. She searched the Bible. She searched the biographies of saints. She searched the lives of others who searched for truth. She withdrew into herself, away from career, friends and the mainstream. It was only when she realized that God had to be put into action—that he wasn't dead, that you couldn't find Him on the pages of a book but that he was Life in action, that he was to be found in the human heart—she began to pick herself up.

She met another mother in a similar situation. Her own heart opened when it went out to this other bruised soul. In order to spread crumbs of comfort, she began to talk about her daughter and actually mentioned the name that had never been uttered since the day Mary died. As she was talking now she realized that Mary had been a big and wonderful part of her life, but even though that part had ended, she was a better human being for having hoped and dreamed and worked for her. "Tragic that it should have ended, but how much better than if it had never existed."

Instead of resenting this mother's drawing on her feeble strength, she suddenly began feeding what turned out to be her own limitless supply.

10

As Miss Hayes put it, "I learned humility and God's pattern finally came clear. Now I know that when he afflicts the celebrated of the world, it is His way of saying, 'None is privileged. In my eyes, all are equal.' "

Mary Baker Eddy said it: "Evil is not supreme. Good is not helpless."

What a great thing to remember when you're ready to give up. It came in pretty handy to flying ace Eddie Rickenbacker, when he and his crew were brought down at sea and took refuge in a rubber raft. They drifted for days without food or water—all of them bordering on insanity, a few of them hysterical, raving.

Rickenbacker began to pray—all alone. His faith was so strong—he prayed continually—and was finally joined by the crew out of desperation. Rick worked on the belief that God's supply is inexhaustible. Wherever we are, the Lord is protecting and caring for us. If we hold fast to that truth and we acknowledge the ever-presence of God and the powers he possesses, our prayers will be answered because God's supply is inexhaustible. Faith is the infinite supply of God.

Suddenly a seagull landed on Rickenbacker's head—a messenger right from God in answer to his prayers. Of course, the crew killed it and ate it. Shortly afterward they were all rescued.

Boy, that Mary Baker Eddy really has something there: *Evil is not supreme. Good is not helpless.*

I was telling this story to a friend who didn't seem to be too enthusiastic. "I tried the prayer bit for years," he said. "It doesn't always work."

"You're a comic," I explained. "You know that timing is very important. You tell a joke and wait for the laughs. Sometimes you have to have a lot of patience—for the laughs *or* the healing."

"Oh," he cried, "if God would only help me—until he helps me!"

"Well," I said, "you have to do something about that yourself. Prayers are not enough. You've got to back it up with faith

. . . and the use of the ability and talent He gave you. You know the story about the priest and the rabbi who were watching the fight at Madison Square Garden. One of the fighters kneeled and crossed himself right before the bell.

"Will that help him?" the rabbi asked.

"If he can punch, it will," the priest answered.

" 'Trust in the Lord with all thine heart; and lead not unto thine own understanding. In all thy ways acknowledge Him, and He shall direct thy path'—but you've got to give Him a little help." And then I hit him with the punchline: "Don't be impatient. Just because you decided now you want something from Him, you think He ought to drop everything and help you—remember, He waited a long time for you to show up."

William Gargan is a perfect example. The former motion picture, TV and stage star "died" back in 1960 when he had to have his larynx removed because of cancer. A devout Catholic, he was "close to the unforgivable sin of despair for a long time."

Bill says, "When I was told that I had the big C, I went straight to hell. I was only fifty-five and I had been on the verge of signing a million-dollar contract for a television series. Just like that it was all over—my career, my life, everything. I suddenly felt very old—actually, I felt dead, although they hadn't gotten around to nailing the lid over my head.

"But with God's help, I came back from all that. I began to realize that as long as I could breathe, there had to be some purpose to my being alive. I couldn't return to acting, but I found a new career, a new life, which I think has been far more meaningful than anything I ever did before."

In his new career he travels around the country addressing speech rehabilitation institutes, Golden-age groups of laryngectomy patients, cancer-control organizations and the like.

"You know," he says, "I don't come up with what you might call dulcet tones—but I have no trouble making myself understood—and I don't pull any punches. I tell them no matter what age they are, they have to exert themselves if they want to talk again, as I did.

"I have to tell you," he adds, "you don't have to be old or have cancer to want to sit back and feel sorry for yourself. Young people in the prime of health do it, too. For them, it's an easy way to drop out of society and evade responsibility. The big cure? Faith!"

I delivered the eulogy when Gladys Hampton, the wife of Lionel Hampton, died in 1971. "I got to call it quits, too," Hamp said to me that sad day. "Gladys was such a big part of me. Now that she's gone, I'll never play another note again. For the thirty-five years of our marriage she was my manager, my bookkeeper, my agent and my preacher. Now, suddenly, she's not here."

Hamp even wanted to throw away his big dream—the housing project and music school he wanted so much to build in poverty-stricken Harlem, an area he had lived in for thirty years. Anyway, the whole idea was running into trouble. Many of the Harlem residents were unhappy that whites were going to do much of the construction and that some whites were even going to the school. The hatred started to rise and poor Hamp, especially in his condition, didn't know how to deal with it. Some residents even threatened to tear down the complex if it was ever built.

"One night," Hamp told me, "I was sitting at home, ready to give it all up, wondering what Gladys would have thought. How I prayed that she were here to give me the answers like she always did. We always shared our joys as well as our troubles. Then I remembered what she usually said when I had a problem: 'Dear, let's forget our worries tonight and rub them out by reading from the Psalms.'

"Gladys's favorite was Psalm 40, the second verse in particular. And that's what I read now. 'He brought me up also out of an horrible pit, out of the miry clay, and set my feet upon a rock, and established my goings.'

"This was the turning point. Right after that I came to life

—like after a four-bar rest. I called, wrote, fought, begged, and went to Harlem to talk to the people there.

"Look," I told them, "it's just like music, you got to have the white keys as well as the black ones to make harmony. They bought it, and before long, black workers were working side by side with white workers and I had, through God's help, pulled myself out of the horrible pit I had caught myself in."

Soon after that Lionel Hampton held a ceremony to open his project. There were parades and bands and speeches. Hamp even jammed himself for the overflowing audience that had come to see his dream come true. The thing that made him proudest of all was the motto that was engraved in front of the buildings. It was that old second verse of the 40th Psalm: ". . . and He set my feet upon a rock—and established my goings."

Sandy Duncan, the star of television's "Funny Face" wasn't always a winner—but her losings are what made her a star.

In the old days, her best friend was her grandpa, Jeff Scott, who she always called Jeff—and she called him often when she was in trouble.

"Jeff loved to tell stories," she says, "and though he was very well read, he was always mixing up his quotes. 'As the Bible says,' he'd tell me, 'to thine own self be true' or 'Ralph Waldo Emerson said a mouthful when he declared that God is our refuge and strength.' Maybe he mixed up the name tags, but the product was always solid. 'You'll get no junk from Jeff,' he used to say—and boy, was he right!"

When Sandy was fifteen, living in Tyler, Texas, and lost out as cheerleader for the football season, she didn't think she would ever get over the hurt. As usual, she ran to grandpa for help and consolation. "Oh, Jeff," she cried, her tears covering her face, "Why? I worked so hard and I wanted so much to win. Why didn't I? This is gonna hurt for a long time—maybe forever."

"Listen, honey," he told her, "I know a proverb you ought to be thinking about. It's only four words, but I've tested them,

14

and they are tried and true. 'No pains—no gains."

"What a lesson," Sandy says now, "and believe me, I needed those four words later in life. I haven't been happy with the sudden closing of my TV show, or the misery of the break-up of my first marriage, or the losing of my left eye, but I do believe these things have made me more aware of living than I ever was—and more grateful. I think I'm more aware of other people and what they are feeling and I know that when I'm thinking of them, I worry less about myself."

Jeff is not around now, but if he's listening, I think his granddaughter could give him a proverb of her own that she discovered: "There's nothing evil about pain—unless it conquers you."

Does the faith bit work? You can bet your life it does! Actually, that's what you're doing when you put your life in His loving hands.

I remember how it worked for me one scary night. I was leaning over my sink when I felt a crack in my back. I couldn't straighten up. I was panic-stricken. I knew from past experience that this meant torture for me. I screamed for Cindy to help me. "I can't get up," I said. "What will I do?"

Cindy just looked at me and said calmly, "The only support you have is from God!"

I stood still for just a moment—and then I just straightened up and walked away. I have never been bothered with this problem again.

Chapter 2.

Pat Boone

In show business circles Pat Boone is known as a square. The word is out that he's a "God nut." Backstage talk is that he's a "faith bug." Show people have dubbed him a "Jesus kook." And those are the people who *like* him!

Don Rickles at various times has introduced him as "Mr. Clean," "Pat Bland," "Goody White Shoes," "the teen-age Billy Graham," and a lot of other things that you'll never hear from a pulpit.

I once introduced Pat at a benefit this way: "He's so religious—on the high holy days he wears stained-glass spectacles." Another time I said, "When St. Peter prays, he prays to Pat Boone."

Phil Harris met our boy on the Andy Williams TV program and said, "You know, Pat, I never had a son, but if I did, I'd want him to be just like you—until he was three years old."

Dean Martin presented Pat on his show in his own inimitable 100-proof way: "That Pat Boone is so religious—I shook hands with him and my whole right side sobered up."

Pat laughs at all of these "compliments" now, but not long ago he was cringing at them. He didn't want to be an oddity

—or a square. He wanted to belong in show business but he didn't want to give up his church, either.

"The more I tried living in two worlds," Pat told me, "the more I found myself pulled apart. I was one Pat Boone in church, another at home, another on television and another at a Hollywood party. As I wondered and wandered, my marriage, my family life, my faith, all began to unravel in the classic tragic pattern of today. My wife didn't love me. My children didn't care. In addition, I had financial problems—serious ones. What I needed was a miracle.

"And the greatest miracle of all hit me. I discovered something more important to me than my public image or what Don Rickles or Phil Harris or Dean Martin said about me—my relationship with the most significant person in all history—Jesus.

"Up to this time I had been a churchman, paying my dues. I'd been investing regularly in the institutional bank: church attendance, contributions and all the rest. The 'treasure' was accumulating in my heavenly account, all right, but I was afraid to write checks on it. In other words, I didn't know how to claim the promises that Jesus makes in the Bible to those who'll believe Him.

"The trouble was, I'd lived in God's house twenty-one years without meeting my landlord! I knew a lot about Him—but now I've met Him!

"I've discovered that Jesus Christ is as alive today as He was two thousand years ago when He walked the dusty roads of Galilee. And man, when you experience His living presence, not just intellectually but in your very spirit—*you know it.* And so, my life has changed."

That's when the greatest miracle of all happened to Pat Boone. "The miracle I saw in my wife's eyes, a light in my kids' eyes, a relationship that carries beyond religion and into every segment of life.

"And for the person who has found this type of faith, it means he is the same person every day, all the time, regardless of whether he is in church, at home, at work or wherever."

Now Pat can laugh when he is heckled on television by his

20

show-business pals. "You don't drink at all?" Phil Harris asked Goody White Shoes on one show.

"That's true," Pat answered.

"You mean, nothing, never, nothing at all?"

"No, Phil, nothing ever."

Turning to the studio audience, Phil said, "Can you imagine waking up in the morning and knowing that's as good as you're gonna feel all day long?"

Everybody howled, including Mr. Clean. Pat could have topped him very easily. "It wouldn't have done anybody any good to have said that I feel great when I wake up—now, more than ever." I have a hot tip for you: that God bit works a lot better and faster than the booze bit ever did.

Pat is now singing "A New Song," which happens to be the title of his book. He talks about his drinking problem, his lost love, his bankrupt business and his mixed-up life but, "Thank God, when I finally admitted my failure and my inadequacy, He restored me into fellowship with Him. And when I gave Him back a life and career that I had thoroughly messed up, He drew me into a greater more powerful relationship to Him than I had ever dreamed possible."

Pat is singing a new song because God is now enabling him to help others through the talents and opportunities He gave him years ago.

"And I want so much to help," Pat says. "Churches today are in a terrible crisis. Young people are rejecting organized religion. They're not buying the comfortable, dogmatic, lethargic, impractical, unwieldly, clannish groups that meet in fancy buildings. They're looking for God! The God of Abraham, Moses, Peter, Paul and Christ! The God of action, of change, the God of now! What the Holy Spirit is doing today is disturbing—disturbing in the same manner that Christ disturbed 'organized religion' and the world two thousand years ago.

"Hundreds of thousands of men and women today are simply reading the Word of God. Then they're thanking Him for it and committing their lives to Him. To them He is proving His immediacy and reality in countless, specific, dramatic and

21

breath-taking ways. And with these 'confirmation contracts' people are receiving joy, purpose and eternal identity!

"The other night as my wife and I prayed, I asked God to do a lot of things—for our family, our friends, our nation and our world. After quite a bit of these requests, I had to say, 'O Father, I ask you for so much, all the time; what is there, if anything, that I can give you?'

"And the answer rose so quickly and forcefully in my spirit as if I heard God say: 'Just give Me you—And I will give you Me!'

"Think of it! Oh, my friends, imagine it! The most preposterously unequal trade in creation! We have only ourselves to give Him, yet two thousand years ago Jesus said, 'For God so loved the world that He gave His only begotten son, that whomever believes in Him should not perish, but have eternal life'—so much for so little.

"This incredible, priceless swap has begun for us. Glory to the living God. He's willing and ready to do the same for you. Will you let Him?"

Chapter 3.

He Is Only a Prayer Away

Prayer is transferring your problem to God, and you don't have to be on your knees or stand on your head to get Him to tune you in. He has had you bugged all the time, way before they thought of it at Watergate—and all you need to have Him listen is the desire—because desire is prayer.

I'll let Walt Disney speak for me: "A prayer implies a promise as well as a request; at the highest level, prayer not only is supplication for strength and guidance but also becomes an affirmation of life and thus a reverent praise of God."

Each of us does it in our own way. The late Secretary General of the United Nations, U Thant, began each day with his alarm going off at six-thirty in the morning and for about fifteen minutes afterward, Thant, a Buddhist, sat quietly in meditation. "I try to shut myself off from all senses and concentrate on my inner self," he said. "You think on what is good in life, good thoughts, good deeds. It is difficult to explain exactly, but it is something like your New Year's resolutions every day."

Prayer is a personal thing. Jesus gave specific instructions on how to pray. He said, "Pray to thy Father which is in secret." You learn from the very beginning that it doesn't work if it's not personal.

I have a friend who learned this the hard way. He walked into his daughter's room one night and asked, "What about your prayers?"

She answered, "I'm saying them."

He said, "I don't hear you."

And the daughter replied, "I'm not talking to *you.*"

Prayer is spiritual communion with God, a deep conviction with oneself of God's presence, goodness and power, and of His great love for humanity.

The big trick is to work it out your own way. Dean Martin says, "Of course I believe in God very much. I still have never missed a night without praying. I still have my St. Christopher and when I get on an airline I cross myself and pray to Him. I don't get on my knees, I pray in bed.

"Oh, I believe in God. I don't understand too many things; for example, when a baby comes from a lady, who's gonna make this thing with the ears and the nose and the mouth and the eyes? Who? Why, God, of course, and when people are scared or in trouble or are hurt, what do they say? 'God help me!' 'Cause who they gonna turn to, Henry Ford?"

Joe Namath says, "Most of my prayers are saying thanks for everything I've got and how can a guy have more? I love my life, and I don't think I'd change places with anyone. I'd trade *knees* with anyone, but not places."

When Joe is too busy or forgets, he lays off his prayers on his mother, who says enough for the whole team. "She's beautiful," Joe says. "When she watches the Jets play on television, she prays to two saints, one when we've got the ball and one when the other team has the ball. She's the only person I know who has an offensive saint and a defensive saint."

James Francis Durante, lovingly called the Schnozzola, believes there are more good people in the world than bad. He says, "I don't mind if a gentleman scratches a match on my furniture, so long as he is careful to go with the grain."

Jimmy Durante starts off each day with a prayer. He wears a crucifix ring on his left hand, and never misses Sunday mass or a day of obligation—but if he's busy, he'll take his confession or prayers any place that's handy.

Once, when he was working at the Copacabana in New York and living at a local hotel, he decided to call Father Bob Perella, the show-business priest, to hear his confession. What better place than the privacy of his bedroom? Father Bob arrived and went right to Jimmy's suite. While Jimmy was talking to somebody on the phone about a picture deal, Fatso Marco, one of Jimmy's second bananas, invited the priest to have a drink. "Sure," he said, "I'll have a nice cold scotch and soda."

When Jimmy finished his call they went into his bedroom to have their talk and say their prayers. Now they are alone. Jimmy is kneeling beside Father Bob, his eyeglasses on his face, a prayer book in his hands. He reverently begins, "Bless me, Father, for I have sinned."

Suddenly the door bursts open and in comes Fatso Marco holding a small tray with the scotch and soda. Durante is flabbergasted. "What kind of a nut are you, Fatso?" he hollered. "Can't you see I'm making my confession?"

Fatso looked Jimmy straight in the eye and answered, "Just because you got problems, the priest has to go dry?"

Father Bob prides himself on his good connections in keeping the show-business fraternity in good shape. He is called on to bless anything from an opening night to a black-tie Bar Mitzvah.

Danny Stradella, the owner of Danny's Hideaway, called Father Bob one day and asked if it wouldn't be too inconvenient, could he please bless his new Eldorado. "I couldn't even think of placing my brand-new Cadillac on any dirty city street unless you first poured some nice, clean holy water on it," Danny said. Of course, the show-business priest blessed the car and they rode away happily.

A couple of weeks later, the priest got a call from Danny's doorman. "Did you hear the news, padre? Danny's car is smashed to bits. Some drunk hit him while he was standing still and it's a complete wreck. I thought you'd like to know."

"And I had just blessed the car," Father Bob told me. "I realize I don't give any guarantees with my blessings, but the poor man—I wonder what Danny will say when he sees me."

That night the priest walked into Danny's. The mere sight of him induced an instant act of thanksgiving. "Thank God you blessed my car that day. If you hadn't, I wouldn't be here talking to you!"

Cecil B. DeMille was a very religious man. His great ambition was to bring the Ten Commandments to the screen. He prayed that he would complete it before he went to his reward. As it turned out, it's very lucky he was prayed up.

While making the picture, he climbed to the top of one of the 103-foot gates, up a perpendicular ladder, a pretty good feat for a man of 75. As he reached the top and looked down on the immense multitude he felt an overwhelming sense of pride.

Suddenly a terrible pain shot through the center of his chest. He staggered and his face turned green. He began to bend over. The pain was worse than anything he ever felt. For a moment he couldn't breathe. The thousands of people below were now a blur.

When his assistant saw this, he tried to help but DeMille brushed him aside. "You can't descend the ladder now," the man warned. "How am I going to get down—fly?" he answered. Mustering his extraordinary will power, praying all the time, and with God's arms around him, he made the descent, then sank to a sitting position.

He rallied again for a few moments, long enough to hear his doctor tell him that he must abandon the direction of the picture. Naturally, he refused.

That night DeMille was carried into his bedroom and he prayed as he had never prayed before in his life. We will never know what he asked God to provide, but it must be that he called upon all the strength that lay within his being, that he was looking to draw up power from the very wellsprings of life itself.

When his wife took his hand the next morning, he knew that he had been spared, his prayers had been answered. *The Ten Commandments* would be completed and his dream come true.

Do you need any more proof of the power of prayer? If you need a topper, here it is. A young sailor was sitting next to me on a plane going to California. "I'm on my way to join my ship in San Diego," he told me. "I almost didn't make it. I tried for a year to get in the Navy, but was turned down because of poor eyesight. Finally, to get rid of me, they told me to go home and eat carrots daily to improve my eyesight. I did just that, and two months later they accepted me in the Navy."

Of course, the carrots didn't heal him or his eyesight. It was his great desire to be cured. Desire is prayer because you're making a plea to the Lord. The carrots didn't have the curative power, but it was his desire to be cured and the faith he put in the carrots.

You just never know where your faith will lead you.

These three little boys were always late for Sunday School, and Father McNulty was told that they played hooky from school a lot, too. He finally got them all together in his study.

"Okay, boys," he said, "let's put our cards on the table. Don't you want to go to heaven?" Two of the boys said sure they did. The third shouted an emphatic no.

"You mean you don't want to go to heaven when you die?" the priest asked.

"Oh, when I die?" the youngster exclaimed. "Of course I do when I die—I thought you were getting up a crowd to go now!"

And as long as we're on a kick about how young people react to God, I should tell you the story of Dick Van Dyke's youngest daughter, Carrie Beth. Dick swears he walked in on her as she was closing her prayers and heard her say, "Good-bye, God, we're going to California."

Once upon a time Peter Lind Hayes and his wife, Mary Healy, were performing in a nightclub. The applause had just died down when a group straight out of a *Bonnie and Clyde* casting call charged in and announced it was a stickup. Mary was in the back and managed to hide. Peter and the band-leader were stuck out front mixing and mingling with the customers. At this moment they quickly sat down at the near-est table which happened to be with a man whom Peter had brushed off just a little while before. The holdup men were going from table to table collecting money. Peter and the bandleader had none on them since they had been performing and were still wearing their stage clothes. They were rigid with fear. What would the guys do when they got to Peter and the bandleader and came up empty? Frozen in fear they just sat and waited and, as each related it later, both were praying for God's help. Cowering there, they prayed as they had never prayed before. They kept on knowing that God was on the job although He seemed invisible.

Their prayers were answered quickly, mostly because the thieves were only a few tables away and this was no time for God to kid around. Not only did God get the message, but even the man with whom they were seated got it. Without a word between them, he dug down, dredged out some money and whispered hoarsely, "Here, take a little." Peter and his pal stuffed it into their pockets and when the holdup men reached them they were able to match the others in making a donation. Peter will always remember how God heard his prayers and sent an angel—this time in the form of a stranger—to answer them.

If anybody tells you that prayer doesn't work, slug 'em—with some of these true stories. I can only tell you that it works for me. Prayer changed my whole life. Let me tell you about it.

The late mayor of New York, Fiorello H. LaGuardia, was my "adopted" father. The Little Flower, as he was affectionately called, was always there to guide me in the right direction when I came to a crossroad. When I ran away from City College for a nightclub job or a vaudeville date, it was LaGuardia who would kick my fanny and then call the dean to take me back. When I was behind in my studies, he would put aside his congressional duties and work with me on my homework until I was caught up.

He was always there at the right time, every step of the way, to build me up when I was low and knock me down when I started to carry on a great love affair—unassisted. "Conceit is God's gift to little men," he told me. "Don't worry about people knowing you," he cautioned. "Make yourself worth knowing."

If I had followed that advice when I opened at the State Theatre in Baltimore, too many years ago, it would have stopped me from walking into lamp posts. The part of my heart that chipped off that fateful weekend took a long time to heal.

I was sixteen years old and full of energy, ambition and loaded with ham. My first professional engagement in a vaudeville theatre almost turned out to be my last. I arrived at the State Theatre in Baltimore with no music, no experience, very little talent and an overabundance of guts.

I tried to hide my inadequacies with bluff, brashness and a phony superiority. When my act died, I screamed at the musicians. I cut up everybody from the stagehands to the manager of the theater. I blamed everyone and everything except my act.

Show people are the warmest in the world. If only I had come to them and explained that this was my first professional job, they would have done everything in the world to help me. Instead, I found myself hated by everybody in the theater, including the audiences. By the third day I was about as popular as a stripper at a DAR convention.

I just wasn't ready. Each show I died a little more. "Those lousy audiences," I kept trying to assure myself, "they must eat their young in this town."

When I came offstage after the last show on the third day I was no longer the flip little guy who was going to kill the people. I ran, sobbing, to my dressing room. I looked in the mirror and saw a frightened little kid with tear stains and smeared makeup. "I'm just a flop—I'm nothing—I'm quitting," I kept telling myself.

It was Christmas Eve and there I was all alone in my dressing room, with no friends or family. A failure as a comedian and a failure as a person. I was ready for the window.

I closed my eyes to blot it all out and then I thought of LaGuardia's words: "Don't worry about people knowing you. Make yourself worth knowing." That's when I started to pray. I must have sat there for fifteen minutes talking to God. When I opened my eyes I saw lights blinking on and off. I was looking at a Christmas tree through my window across the street. "That's it," I hollered, "that's it—my prayers are answered."

I dug my hands in my pocket. My palm revealed that I was worth $1.85. "I can do it for that," I muttered.

I quickly put on my street clothes and ran to everybody backstage, inviting them to my Christmas party. I was no longer the fresh little punk who barked orders at stagehands and insulted musicians. I invited the electricians, the prop men, the musicians, as well as the other acts on the bill. They all thanked me politely and most of them said they would come.

I was happy for the first time since I arrived in Baltimore. I walked into a big supermarket next door to the theater. For a dollar I bought more potato chips, peanuts, pretzels and popcorn than I could carry. Ten cents went for paper plates.

I rushed back to my room with the stuff and started setting the food out on the mantlepiece and the chairs. There were a dozen paper plates in the carton, and after heaping each one full of popcorn, potato chips, peanuts and pretzels, I still had enough of these poor man's hors d'oeuvres for another round.

I stepped back to survey my display. Maybe it's not much, I thought, but at least it's beginning to look like Christmas. If only I had a tree.

I put my hand in my pocket and drew out seventy-five cents. All I had left in the world. I jumped into my hat and coat and took the steps three at a time. I ran into the street looking for my tree. I finally came to a store that had the remnants of a Christmas sale. There were only a few trees left. I blew my entire capital on a skinny, bare hunk of scraggly foliage that was naked six inches from the top.

By the time I got the tree home, I felt a little ashamed of it. It looked even more anemic now than it had in the store. I had no money left at all for decorations.

Again, I donned my hat and coat and ran backstage to the deserted theater. I rummaged through the big garbage box and came up with dozens of empty cigarette packages, some old ribbons from Christmas packages that had been opened backstage and some gold foil from holiday cigars.

When I arrived home I meticulously stipped the tin foil of the cigarette packages and tied the strips to a number of branches. I did the same with the gold foil. Then I spliced the ribbon and draped it around the other branches. I took the gold pen and pencil my mom had given me for my graduation and hung it on the tree.

Then I stood back to view my handiwork. The tin foil, the gold foil, the colored ribbon and the gold pen and pencil actually gave the withered pine some semblance of life.

Not bad, I thought. I glanced at my watch: 10:30. They should be coming pretty soon. I put my watch on the tree and sat down to wait. I picked up the Bible that was in my room and started to read it.

It was 11:30 when I looked again and no one had shown up yet. "They probably stopped off to have a drink," I told myself. "They should be here any minute."

After another fifteen minutes that seemed like fifteen years, I started to pace the floor. They wouldn't do this to me. Not all of them—at least some of them will show.

By now it was almost midnight. "What am I kidding myself for?" I cried. "If anybody were coming, they'd have been here an hour ago. I guess I'm just a punk kid to them. Not good enough to share Christmas with—the lousy bums—I'll never talk to them again—I won't even spit on them—those phonies—"

I looked at the tree. In my bitterness, the Christmas glow

33

was gone. Now I saw it for what it really was: A consumptive-looking little growth with some garbage on it. The sight of the popcorn and the peanuts made me sick.

I thought of the past three days since I had left New York. Of my complete failure on the stage and off. And now, sitting alone in my lonely little room on Christmas Eve, with not a soul bothering to show up at my party.

This fate was a little too much for a sixteen-year-old. My head started to pound, my chest filled until I could hardly breathe and my whole frame shook as I sobbed uncontrollably.

Suddenly I sat up. I thought I heard someone knocking at the door. I muffled my sobs and listened. Yes, there was someone knocking. I tried to cover up my sobbing and my voice came out so high only dogs could hear me. "Just a minute."

Hurriedly, I poured some water in the basin and pushed my face into it. While wiping my face with the towel, I nonchalantly opened the door.

A group of people, laden with bundles, stood in the darkened hallway. Before I knew what was happening, my little room was overflowing with hams, turkeys, candies, bottles, gaily wrapped packages and happy, laughing people. The entire cast was there, and all the people from the theater.

A little man stepped out of the darkness. He was carrying an armful of packages that seemed to touch the sky.

"Merry Christmas, son," said the Little Flower.

The effectual fervent prayer of a righteous man availeth much. I wish I could take credit for that line, but I must admit I stole it from the Bible—James 5:16.

As a matter of faith, some of the greatest stories of all time come out of the Bible, as well as the Koran, the Talmud, and the Christian Science texts.

"The prayer that reforms the sinner and heals the sick is an absolute faith that all things are possible to God,—a spiritual understanding of Him, an unselfed love." This is the very first sentence of the first chapter of *Science and Health with Key to the Scriptures*, by Mary Baker Eddy.

Carol Channing uses this prayer every day of her life and

lives by it. "The saddest people in the world," says Carol, "are the people who do not believe. They are those people who do not care—the salesman who is curt, the actress who throws away a performance, the student who turns in a hastily prepared assignment. Why is it that the salesman doesn't understand that it is he, not the customer, who loses by a lost sale?

"I think that people who do care are the happy people—having concern for and deep feelings about—has a way of enlarging your existence. It makes you apply yourself, and the more time you devote to caring about people and principles, the less room there is for gloom."

Carol learned from her father that a person who cares, *really* cares for his God, leads a life loaded with hard work and with contentment. "Lynn Fontanne once told me that she gives her best performance when she doesn't feel like going onstage and has to reach to heaven to get through," Carol says. "That's because she cares. And if you care, nothing is too tough to do. My father, when he talked to God used to say, 'Please, Lord, give Carol a task too big for her to handle.'"

All of us have nights when we go onstage and the audience is cold. (I know you won't believe it, but it even happens to me —often.) There are plenty of nights I have had to "reach to heaven" to get laughs.

Carol has a great little trick she uses: 'I care about your having a good time tonight,' she says to herself as she faces the audience. 'I know you've been working hard and you're all tired out. You've had a big dinner and you've paid a lot of money for your seats, so I'll do my best to make you happy.' You want to know something? It works.

"As I put myself in their place and feel for them," Carol explains, "as individually as possible, before you know it, the laughter is coming and down over the orchestra pit comes a bridge of love that you could walk over. That's because they know I care about them."

A lot of people say that the ability to care or feel for somebody else besides yourself is a gift, something you are born with like a sense of humor or rhythm or ESP.

"That's not true," Carol says. "I believe we are born loving

35

and charitable creatures, but that along the way we learn to be lazy and to be afraid, and yes, even hate, and somehow our true feelings become submerged. I believe that people simply lose contact with the God who created them.

"That contact can be reestablished with prayer. We can reach out to God directly, as my father did, devoting his life fully to his religion or we can make contact indirectly, reaching him through others, by consciously doing for others. It's when we take the plunge we've been too afraid to take, deliberately putting ourselves in other people's shoes, involving ourselves in their struggles, that indifference falls away and an exciting feeling of concern takes over. That's caring."

Columnist Hy Gardner says, "Actors aren't people, though there are plenty of people who are actors." In the world of illusion, false hair, false eyelashes, false noses and false hopes, you learn to hang onto that which is real. The pure and simple fact is that in the world of make-believe, God has always been a headliner.

God is out there with you. He loves it when you're active —glorifying Him. You can bet He's watching over you when you're doing your thing. I saw one actor get out onstage and finish his performance without knowing it happened. Not until he got to his dressing room, after the show, and noticed his clothes soaked with blood, did he realize he had been cut and needed twelve stitches.

It shows only that a human being should do what he's supposed to do—get up out of bed and work. When I appeared in *Guys And Dolls,* there was one of the stars who was in an accident and had a very bad limp. I was worried about his making the show. But he was determined that the show must go on. He limped to the entrance—but when he walked onstage he was perfect.

I have seen stutterers and stammerers sing and speak beautifully as soon as the spotlight hit them. I have seen coughers and sneezers clear up the moment they hit the podium.

Eddie Albert put it pretty well: "To think that we can

accomplish anything on our own—without God's help—is naive." I know Jesus won't mind Eddie switching it from His original: "I can of myself do nothing—"

I guess that's what we're all striving to do, show people as well as civilians, find a rapport with God—somebody who can watch over us—and then we've got it made.

Jim Nabors's parents sacrificed and worked hard to bring up and educate their children. Jim's goal in life was to amount to something big and pay back his parents—to make them proud—but he was a failure in everything he tried.

Then he found himself suddenly drawn to attend services in a church near his home in Hollywood—and suddenly he found a new meaning and importance in life—far greater than his own ambitions. He became devoted to his God and His teachings.

With the change came a new attitude and on he went to become one of the TV greats. Jim has not stopped thanking God with special prayers every day, for showing him this new way of life.

Jackie Gleason first met God through his mother. "My father disappeared when I was eight years old," the Great One says, "and Mother went to work as a change-maker in the subway.

"You see, my mother was a very religious woman who suffered all the indignities, after my father left, of being on her own with a tough little kid on her hands.

"One of my most vivid memories was when I belonged to the Catholic Boys Brigade, which required a uniform which cost seven dollars. I don't know where Mom got the money—but I had my uniform. She must have done without for herself for a long time to pay for it. One morning when the snow was thick on the ground and I was watching her dress to get ready for work, I saw her put on my leggings—and then her stockings over them.

"Until then I had been a terror—but that morning I got

on my knees and prayed to God that I would be a good or anyway what I thought was a good boy—to pay her back for all her sacrifices."

Beverly Sills, the great opera star, was practically born with faith. "As a child I remember a certain ritual my mother and I would share as I went off to school," she recalls. "She would give me three kisses and I would say, 'Mama, pray for me.' I still, to this very day, will phone her anytime during the day or night and ask her, 'Before you go to bed, Mama, take care of this for me, will you?' I'll tell her the problem and then say, 'Pray hard,'—and we both do."

The opera star needed a lot of prayers when her children were born. Muffy was dumb and almost totally deaf and Bucky was an epileptic. When doubt and despair hit her worst, she would phone her mother, as always, to ask her to help her pray. Beverly Sills recounted, " 'In God's sight,' Mom would say, 'your children are perfect—no flaws. We must see them as He does.' One day she scolded me. "Why do you try to carry the whole world on your shoulders? Leave some of it to God. Don't you know that he's eager to help you?' "

That's when Beverly Sills decided to go out and help others. A kind of freedom came to her—an end to her bitterness. She found herself lecturing to mothers with retarded children. "Mothers with the same despairing look on their faces that I used to have," she says. "I speak to them frankly about what will happen to their babies. 'We already know what happens to the mothers,' I say with a smile. 'We get prematurely old.' "

Beverly Sills is a star in every sense of the word. She has found joy even in sadness, because she is helping others. "I believe," she says, "that God is not some uncaring force; I believe He hurts when we hurt, because He loves us. If I didn't feel this way I couldn't talk to Him the way I do. Nor could I thank Him for helping me to rediscover joy and to pass it on to others."

Duke Ellington says, "God gives each of us a role to play in life—mine is music. I have written thousands of pieces, many of them called sacred music.

"Where do they come from? God fills your mind and your heart with them. All you have to do is believe and wait until they come and use them, whether it's laying a brick a new way or writing a song."

Every man prays in his own way and his own language. There is no language that God doesn't understand. The sacred music that Duke writes is an act of worship. "I'm only saying in music," he says, "what I have been saying on my knees for a long time."

The Agent in the Sky found Glenn Campbell in Billstown, Arkansas, and put him in the big time. If you've got it and you believe, the Greatest Talent Scout of them all will find you wherever you are.

Glenn was one of twelve children and it was a struggle. "We were poor," Glenn says, "but our home was full of love. We never missed church on Sundays. We had to get cleaned up, and that meant taking our weekly baths. We didn't have Sunday clothes, so, after our baths we'd put on the same old blue jeans back again and in summer we'd even go to church barefooted.

"But we were grateful for everything. And never afraid or worried about the future. We Campbells grew up knowing that God the Almighty was with us all the time. I realize that the security I felt as I left home didn't just come from having grown up in a cocoon of warm family love: It also came from knowing that God was going to be there watching me wherever I went."

Isn't that a nice thing to hear? What a good lesson for people who are scared—or worry too much—especially those who say they believe. They must have a pretty rotten idea of God's power if they feel so shaky in his hands.

Glenn says he tries to bring up his children with the same kind of love he found in Billstown. "They may have advantages

I never had at home," Glenn says, "but as I take them to Sunday school now I can say to myself, 'Yes, they can get the same sense of security I got—even with their Sunday clothes and shoes on.'"

God covers Billstown, on his rounds, as well as Washington, D.C., although sometimes it doesn't seem like it. Which reminds me of a story:

The tourist asked the Capitol guide about the man with the collar who seemed to be in a hurry. "He's the chaplain of the Senate."

"Really? Does he pray for the Democrats or the Republicans?" the man wanted to know.

"Well," the guide explained, "he stands before the senators—and prays for the country."

Like The Man says, there is joy in prayer. You can live in a tent or a palace and He will find you—if you really want to be found.

Chapter 4.

John Wayne

"I'll never forget that day. That black day. The day the doctors told me I had 'the Big C,'" said John Wayne. "Ever since I heard those words I haven't quite gotten over the feeling that I'm pretty much living on borrowed time."

It was early in 1965 that the rootin', tootin', shootin' movie hero, who singlehandedly has routed every villain in his 200 films, was cast in a real-life drama. Those of us who've seen him since can testify that he's playing this role with the same four-star heroism that made him one of the top box-office attractions of all time.

Wayne is big and tough. He's a fighter. When he played college football he was the reason the opposition backs never went through tackle. After graduating from the University of Southern California he had to fight to learn his trade. He was a gangling prop boy who "never knew what to do with my hands" when John Ford rewarded him with a film job because he was the only gutsy kid who volunteered to perform a dangerous trick for the camera after a professional stuntman had lost his nerve and chickened out of doing it.

Wayne is used to a rough fight. In some way or other he's

had one all his life. "When the doctor told me what this was and that I would have to have part of a lung removed, it was like a kick right in the face," he explained grimly. "It's a terrible shock. I mean, I can tell you right off that I went black. I knew sure as hell that I didn't want to die yet. I just wasn't ready. I'm still not!

"It's just basically that the word 'cancer' is an awfully frightening word. It terrifies you. It gives you the same terrible feeling that the chilling term 'leprosy' used to."

Wayne was asked if he would have preferred not to know the diagnosis and he answered sharply, "No. I'm not the sort to back away from a fight. Any fight. I don't believe in shrinking away from anything. It's not my speed. I never flinched before in my life so I see no reason to do so now. I'm a guy who meets adversities head-on. I face 'em. Had the choice been mine to make, I'd have insisted on knowing right away.

"Frankly, I'm glad they told me. Walking around with this sort of knowledge kind of makes you appreciate things more. You even gaze at the sunrise with a little more enjoyment. Suffering gives you a better perspective, and you somehow feel a lot more gratitude for every little thing than you ever used to before.

"By the same token, I'm too forthright a fella to keep this hidden from anybody else because of fear, either. All my advisers begged me to conceal this illness on the grounds that it would hurt my image. Baloney. I couldn't go along with that way of thinking. It's too phony."

It was at Cine Citta studios in Rome that my wife, Cindy, and I were talking to the Duke. This has been Wayne's nickname since his first boyhood dog, a huge hound, was called "Duke" and he—little Marion Michael Morrison, the pharmacist's son of Winterset, Iowa—was first labeled "Little Duke." Little Duke grew mushroomed into a 6'4" big-boned, broad-shouldered jolly giant, but the nickname remains.

We were sitting quietly, just the three of us, off to a side on the bustling set of *Cast A Giant Shadow,* the war film he and Kirk Douglas were grinding out for United Artists. In front of us, across the hot, steamy road, was the barbed wire of

44

"Dachau." Behind us lay a "forest." In the forest, hundreds of uniformed "GI's" squatted on camp chairs, movie equipment and stumps of trees.

As a prop man hosed down the road so there wouldn't be so many clouds of dust to interfere with the shooting and as Wayne waited patiently to be called, he talked about God. God to him was a friend who embodied all the qualities that he liked in a friend: warmth, understanding, humor. The Duke didn't speak of Him fearfully or tremulously or in whispers. He spoke about Him in the same straightforward, honest, albeit irreverent way he approaches all of life.

"I tell you, honey," he said to Cindy, "even before I got hit with this I always had a pretty high regard for That Man Up There. It isn't like now I'm in trouble so I suddenly discovered Him. No such thing. I always knew about That Fella Upstairs. Oh, sure, there are times you get a little weak because, although it says we're made in the image and likeness of God, the Bible doesn't say we're made in the strength of God. But it's only human to fall down sometimes. He understands that. And he forgives it, too!

"However, I've got to admit that I *really* have a big feeling for The Big Man nowadays. When the world fell in on me, the truth of the matter is I learned to make His acquaintance a little more. Tell you one thing—I was sure talking to Him double-time all of a sudden!"

Wayne grinned broadly then chuckled aloud. "And, believe you me, I know He heard me because I'm here!"

Even handsomer off-screen, John Wayne is so kindly and eager to trade a grin that he's reminiscent of a hopeful scratching his way up instead of a celluloid annuity who has tasted stardom ever since Raoul Walsh, the famous director, changed the Duke's name back in the early 30s. During his short stay in Rome (it was to be five days, but delayed schedules plus a few days in the hospital after wrenching his back in a wrestling scene with Kirk stretched it to two weeks), he was besieged with interview requests. Whatever ones he granted, he did graciously.

He had a smile and a nice word for everyone. "Hell," he

laughed, "I'm not the type to spend time discussing the faults of folks. I like to find their virtues. I like comradeship, camaraderie." As we sat under our tree, a wardrobe girl came over and pinned three stars on his jacket shoulder.

"I don't think so, honey," said Wayne gently. "In this scene we're in combat, and battlefield generals wear their insignia on the inside shirt collar—not in full view. The theory is that if a highranking officer is easily discernible, the enemy will aim for him instead of a private, right?"

Whether the signorina understood English or not, I don't know, but she just kept pinning on his rank silently and determinedly.

"Okay, honey," smiled 'Lt. General' Wayne pleasantly, "I think you're wrong, but if you insist . . ."

Then he turned to me and explained his nature. "I don't make fusses about anything. If I have any real beef, I'll take the director off to a side and tell him calmly. But I always listen to their side and take direction. What the hell, I've done things that directors wanted which I knew was wrong, but if they insist on their position then I let it go. Of course, in *Cast A Giant Shadow*, my son Mike is the co-producer, so I don't dare have too many beefs to begin with."

Around his neck hung a solid gold chain with a gold Jewish star dangling off the end of it.

"How come?" I asked.

"One of my real best friends in the world is a Jew," he answered, "and he said to me recently, 'Okay, Duke, if your time comes, I want you to be ready just in case you're going to have to slip in the back door.' I figure he has a good point, so I've worn his present ever since he gave it to me.

"I'm innately a God-fearing man," he'll tell you. "I was born Catholic. My parents saw to it that I was spoon-fed my catechism as a boy, but as I've added a few years I've grown away from the actual dogma a lot. I haven't grown away from the uplifting faith, but I have pulled away from the entangling religion.

"I guess what could be said about me now is that I'm a cardiac Catholic. To put it simply, this means that I've got it

46

down deep in my heart even if I don't practice its tenets or subscribe to the creeds. Tell you something else—to be perfectly honest, just because I'm here in Rome doesn't make me have any desire to visit the Pope. Now, if that's a sin, then I'm sorry. But everything's a sin someplace. I'm a fella who likes to belt whiskey. However, the Baptists think it's wrong to do that. And the Mormons also frown on whiskey. Look, I have respect for the Pope and for Catholicism and for all religions, but when they put human rules and regulations in place of love for God then I just don't get the message that way!

"I believe in God and I have great reverence for Him, but it's for sure I could never be a deep Catholic. First of all, I've been married three times. Besides that, I dearly adored my grandparents. They had a beautiful life and love together. Their adoration for one another was a touching inspiration to anyone who knew them. Nonetheless, just because the old man was once married before, that meant my grandmother, who was a very devout, very strong Catholic, was forced to lose her position in the church. I don't understand that way of teaching mankind the Good Book. To me, religion should give you life and strength, not take it away."

A woman came by and filthied up his olive-drab uniform by daubing him with a cheesecloth bag filled with dirt. When she left I asked whether his was a charmed life and whether or not his was the first major setback he's ever known.

"I've had many difficulties before," he sighed. "Maybe not one big, overwhelming one like this, but lots and lots of little ones. Everybody has troubles. If it isn't health worries, it's personal worries or career worries or money worries or children worries. There's always something. Life is full of it. Don't tell me just because a guy makes movies, people don't think he's real and human and has problems just like they do. I've had my share, but I've also learned that trouble enriches you. It develops your character. Remember, I said I had a feeling for That Man Upstairs, but He can't do it all alone. He needs help. That's where man's basic nature steps in.

"I was the first guy to make wide-screen pictures and I flopped with them because in those days it was so advanced that nobody even had a theater to play them. But I never whined. I've made more lousy movies than anybody, but I didn't let it get me down. I just kept making so many more of all kinds that nobody even noticed the bad ones anymore.

"I've had my pound of personal unhappinesses, too, and some of those dirty gossip sheets have made it tough on me at those times. After a while you get used to it. When one filthy scandal magazine had something unpretty about my wife and her ex-husband, it was such a horrible business that in a blinding rage, her ex shot the reporter. It wasn't a pleasant episode for me to live through, but when newspapermen badgered me for my comment, you know what I said? 'I'm sorry he was such a poor shot!' I've never been a whiner. I won't be one now."

Wayne took a look around, fell silent for a moment then, "I'm grateful to God right now for giving me a reprieve. I don't know why He lets me hang around. Maybe it's to give me spiritual strength. Maybe He wants to teach me to live a certain way. Maybe it's because He thinks I don't have things set up in the right way yet for my kids . . . who knows . . . I don't know.

"As to the effect this illness had on me with regard to my life, I think that after I got over the initial shock, it was sort of interesting watching human nature at work. When I told everyone I had the 'Big C,' I studied them all to see their reactions. I distinctly remember telling Hal Wallis that I needed to take an extra six weeks because I was going into the hospital. He asked me what for. I told him what for. Then Wallis said, 'Jeez, you can have all the time you want,' and that's when he developed that same facial expression as I guess I had when the doc first hit me with the news.

"Listen, no matter how things go I have no intention of complaining. The Big Man's been mighty good to me. Sure, it was a little tough to breathe with half a lung out, but now I don't notice it. And I *won't* notice it."

Just then the Duke was called to climb into a jeep alongside Kirk Douglas, who was pretending to drive it. (Actually, the jeep was being hauled by another vehicle carrying the camera and lights.) As he left he added, with a twinkle in his

48

eyes, "Maybe, though, I should go to church one day soon. Even if it's only to get my faith jacked up a little. At a time like this it can't hurt."

Amen, Duke!

Chapter 5.

And a Little Child Shall Lead Them

My neighbor's sixteen-year-old son was driving away in his mother's car. "Have a good time," his mom said lovingly.

"Don't tell me what to do," he shouted back.

My friend Harry Hershfield has a solution for these children: "Slap your child every day. If you don't know why—he does."

My brother says, "I never strike my child—except in self-defense."

One lady once told Billy Graham that all her little boy needed was a pat on the back. He answered, "If it was low enough and hard enough, it might do him some good."

It was the Duke of Windsor who remarked, "America is a wonderful place— It's where the parents obey their children."

I don't know. I think the answer is simple. Parents should have a heart-to-heart talk with their children—they'll learn plenty.

"Train up a child in the way he should go; and when he is old, he will not depart from it." I hope you don't mind my lifting that from the Bible (Proverbs 22:6), but it's the real answer.

If you give the child, "the faith as a grain of mustard seed" he will bring you only joy; and prayer is a joyful activity. My friend Isaiah pronounced that the Spirit of the Lord God was upon him not only to comfort all that mourn but to give them, "the oil of joy."

Whatever our religious beliefs, we need all the sense of humor we can gather to appreciate the joy of watching our youngsters grow into their faith.

Dick Van Dyke, who used to be a Sunday-School teacher says, "For that job you must have the wisdom of Solomon, the patience of Job, the courage of David. You must teach like St. Paul, lead like Moses, and stay cool under fire like Shadrach."

One six-year-old boy was reprimanded by his Sunday-School teacher. "You've been nothing but trouble," he said to the youngster. "You're just a rotten kid."

The little boy answered, "That's not true. God made me and he didn't make no junk."

A teacher asked her Sunday-School class to tell the story of creation. One little girl raised her hand with the answer. "First, God created Adam. Then he looked at him and said, 'I think I would do better if I tried again.' So, He created Eve."

"And now, children, who can tell me what we must do before we can expect forgiveness of sin," the teacher asked.

"Well," said little Simon, "first, we've got to sin."

You'll never be able to top the story of the seven-year-old little girl who was sent up to bed after dinner. "Say good night to all our guests," her mom told her, "and don't forget to say your prayers."

"Okay," said the child. "Anybody need anything?"

This youngster came home from Sunday School and his father asked what he had learned. "The Rabbi told us a wonderful story," the kid said, "about the Jews that were chased out of Egypt and they came to the Red Sea. When they saw the

Egyptians following them, they built a bridge over the Red Sea and went over in safety. But when the Egyptians kept coming, they put dynamite under the bridge and when all the Egyptians came on top of the bridge, the Jews blew up the bridge and the Egyptians fell in the Red Sea and were drowned."

"The Rabbi told you this story?" the father asked incredulously.

"No," the kid answered, "but if I told you what the Rabbi told me, you'd never believe it."

"Do you say your prayers before eating?" the teacher asked the little seven-year-old.

"It ain't necessary," she answered. "My mom is a good cook."

One little boy who was given a spanking by his father for dirtying up the house, ran to his mother crying, "Mommie, you should have married Jesus. He loves little children."

My neighbor's little girl has a special prayer: "Please, God, make the bad people good—and the good people nice."

The Hebrew teacher decided to let his class out early. "That's all for today," he announced, "I have a bad headache."

"Oh, I know about that," said little six-year-old David. "Moses had a headache, too."

"Moses had a headache?" the teacher asked. "Where did you hear that?"

"Grandpa told me—he said God gave Moses two tablets."

The clergyman was telling his guests a story when his little girl interrupted: "Daddy," she asked, "is that true—or is that preaching?"

One little boy I know was pretty bad one day, so his father gave him a bit of a spanking and sent him to his room without supper. "And don't forget to say your prayers," he was told. And the old man went to his room to see that he did. The

55

youngster did as he was told. He gave his usual blessings to his family, his friends, his teacher—everybody but his father. Then he turned to his pop and said, "I suppose you noticed you wasn't in it."

The kid came home from Sunday School and the father asked him what he learned today. "The Rabbi taught us Kaddish," the kid said proudly.

"Kaddish?" the old man yelled. "That's a prayer for the dead. You made a mistake." They went to the Rabbi and the father asked him, "What are you teaching my boy?"

"Kaddish," the Rabbi answered.

"But, Rabbi," the father was hysterical, "he's got a father —I'm strong like a horse—he's got a mother—What do you mean you're teaching my boy Kaddish—the prayer for the dead?"

"Don't worry," the Rabbi answered, "you should live so long till he learns it."

My mother-in-law was teaching Sunday School and asked the youngsters to write out the Ten Commandments. When it came to the Fifth Commandment, one boy put down, "Humor they father and thy mother."

The pretty little girl was making her very first appearance in church. "How did you like it?" the preacher asked after the services.

"Well," she answered, "the music was nice—but the commercial was too long."

Rabbi Rabinowitz was a strict teacher and insisted on the best efforts of his pupils. When little David handed in a poor paper, he was furious.

"This is the worst Jewish composition I have ever read," he shouted. "I never saw so many errors. I can't understand how one person could have made all these mistakes."

"One person didn't," David answered calmly. "My father helped me."

I'd like to tell you one of the sweetest stories of all. A mother tells it about her five-year-old daughter who slipped on the rug in her living room and hit her head real hard. It was a pretty rough blow and she began to cry.

Mom comforted her as she applied cold compresses to the lump which had already appeared on her head. Pretty soon the tears stopped and the little girl ran off to play.

That night, after dinner, Mom went to her little girl's room to tuck her in, just in time to hear her prayers. Always after "Now I lay me down to sleep—," she had a special prayer —always about something different—in which she thanked God for "the nicest thing that happend today." It could be the movie she saw—or the double scoop of ice cream—or a car ride or the snow.

This particular night when her mom asked, "What do you want to thank God for tonight?" she answered, "For my bump."

"Why do you want to thank Him for that?" her mother asked.

"Because now He can make it well." With that she gave her mother a kiss, rolled over and closed her eyes.

Mom just sat there thinking, "Yes, God, how often we forget to thank You for the rough, hard times. But it's through them that we often learn the greatest lessons of Your healing love."

Thank you, God, for the bumps.

I heard a story once about a little boy who was having trouble lifting a very heavy stone. His father came along and asked, "Are you using all your strength?"

"I sure am," the boy said.

"No, you're not," the father answered, "I'm right here waiting—and you haven't asked me to help you."

Isn't that a great thing to remember, kids? When we are faced with a pretty rough problem that seems impossible to solve—or a burden too heavy for us to carry—we can ask ourselves: Are we using all our strength? Our Father, too, is waiting to help us.

The best explanation of why there is only one God came from a little boy of eight. "If God fills all space and all places and God is all in all—it's too crowded—there is no room for any other God."

Chapter 6.

———•⚬∞⚬•———

And It Came to Pass

Every time I bumped into this old actor he surprised me with his cheerfulness. I knew he hadn't worked in years. I was aware of the unusual amount of trouble and heartaches he had suffered lately. "How is it," I asked him, "that you always have such a happy disposition? What's the secret?"

"Well," he answered, "the secret of my success—still is—but the Bible says often, 'And it came to pass,' never, 'It came to stay.'"

Paul Harvey says, "Someday I hope to enjoy enough of what the world calls success so that if somebody will ask me, 'What's the secret of it?' I shall say this: 'I get up when I fall down.'"

My friend Herschel Bernardi really had it made. Three hits in a row, "Peter Gunn," *Fiddler On The Roof,* and "Arnie." He was rich, a star, had a beautiful home and a happy marriage.

Suddenly he lost his voice. He needed a throat operation. And that's when the stage opened up and he fell into the pit. It all happened so fast, he didn't even have time to talk it over with the Big Manager. His marriage broke up, the show he was starring in, *Zorba,* closed, he lost his home, his voice was gone and he had no place to go but down. When he hit bottom, and he couldn't go any lower, he picked himself up and went to Mexico and sat on a hilltop.

"Because I couldn't talk," Herschel told me, "I was able to listen. And boy did the Man Upstairs give me an earful. You know if you depend on man, you get what man can do. But if you depend on prayer, you get what God can do. I just decided to depend on prayer.

"As I sat on that hilltop and looked at myself, my whole life came before me, like a man going down for the last time. I realized that losing my voice wasn't so bad after all. Eighty-five percent of what I was saying wasn't worth saying anyway. We spend so much time with baloney and drive and life-and-death options and trying to make good, we don't have time to listen to God or love or enjoy our lives.

"I got a feeling right there that I died and was born again. How important is money? God must hate money—he gave it to so many miserable people. Anyway, the Big Boss doesn't measure people by their fame or their fortune or the part in their last movie. When God measures man, he puts the tape around his heart—not his head or wallet.

"From then on I was free. When I realized that the play is not the thing—it's not life and death—only God can give you that, I knew I had found myself and was home free.

"The first thing I did when I got my voice back was to go to the Wailing Wall in Jerusalem and fall on my knees and thank God that I got a second chance. Now I know who I am. The wall is my home. I know where I belong."

Right now Herschel Bernardi is living quietly on a farm in Columbia, California. "I wake up with the birds singing at my window, and they're not coughing. The trees and the sky and the fresh water surrounds me—and I'm so happy that I can afford it all and that I found out in time that it is in solitude that we hear the voice of God—and brother, I'm listening as hard as I can. At last I know who I am."

"You are God's perfect child," Steve Allen says. "Men usually take pride in the things for which they are least responsible," says Steve, "their looks, their wealth, their social position. But even men of genius or great talent cannot be rightfully proud. For their gifts are God-given.

"God is love, or is God electricity? I do not know what God is—all I hope is that He knows who I am. Electric force can be both measured and diminished—love cannot. At least not in that way. Love is a magic force that knows no laws. A well without a bottom—a purse that's never empty—and love is God and God is love.

"Any measure of success that man attains—remember, it is God-given. Like your fingers and toes and the power of breathing."

That's the secret. To know who you are. It gives you confidence and strength and you could never be afraid again—because you know that the Power behind you is much greater than the problem before you.

Now, take the case of one of the greatest fighters in the history of the ring—Tony Canzoneri. He made millions as a boxer and was five times world champion, but now he was broke and he was joining my show.

It was his debut as a performer and we were getting fifty dollars for four days to break in our act. After three weeks of rehearsing, Tony showed up five minutes before the curtain that first morning. I was furious—or as furious as you can get with a five-time champ. "Where the hell were you?" I screamed. "We go on in five minutes—aren't you nervous?"

"Nervous?" he asked quietly. "Why should I be nervous? I fought a guy called Barney Ross that could knock your head off with a right or a left. There were 20,000 people at Madison Square Garden who paid to come to see me and millions more listening in. I got $250,000 for the fight and I slept for three hours before the fight and I wasn't nervous.

"Here I'm getting a dollar and a quarter a show, there are eleven people in the audience and I can lick every one of them

—including the ushers—so what do you want me to be nervous about?"

And it came to pass—that the beautiful and talented Dorothy Malone was in a fight for her life. The operation lasted eleven hours. When she finally regained consciousness, her mother told her that thousands of people were praying for her recovery.

At first Dorothy thought her mother was saying that to encourage her, but when the letters and telegrams started pouring in and when she saw the newspaper stories that churches of all denominations were holding services for her, she had to believe it—and with belief came a great wave of relief and gratitude.

"You can bet that those prayers all helped," Dorothy says now. "A metaphysician might say that prayer is a form of love, and that love is a healing force. A devout person might say that God hears and answers—it's as simple as that. All I know is that it brings strength and peace when they're needed most."

Friends and fans asked her later if her narrow escape from death made her appreciate life more. Did it make her more religious? Did it bring her closer to God?

Her answers were a gentle, "No—no it didn't make me appreciate life more—because I've always loved life. And, no —not more religious—I've always been religious, and no, it didn't change my relationship with God, it just confirmed it."

Dorothy Malone has always believed. What her illness did was to strengthen and deepen her convictions.

"One of the old clichés in show business," Dorothy says, "is the 'eternal triangle.' Everybody is aware of its meaning. But I've always felt that the most fundamental triangle situation in human affairs is not a situation involving a man and two women, or a woman and two men. For me, the only truly eternal triangle is the relationship between one person and another person and God—with God at the apex of the triangle.

"Certainly, in the case of the people who were kind enough to pray for me during my illness, this 'eternal triangle' was very much in evidence. And I'm convinced that the benefits flow in all directions, on all sides of the triangle, so that those who pray are helped as well as those who are prayed for.

"This is not something I learned from my illness. It's a conviction that was deepened and strengthened by it. This concept of the eternal triangle has become an inseparable part of my life."

All of us pray overtime when, "it comes to pass," and we don't want it to stay. And each one of us has his own way of making it work:

Humorist Sam Levenson says, "My wife and I and our children like to believe that God dwells in our house, so we feel it is only proper that on the Sabbath we should return the courtesy of visiting Him in His house."

Pearl Bailey says, "My church is where I am. See this ground? This is my floor. Do you see the mountains? They are my walls. And the sky? That is the ceiling of my church."

The Indian has his own way: "Please, Great Spirit, help me never to judge another until I have walked two weeks in his moccasins."

The beloved Eleanor Roosevelt always carried this prayer with her: "Our Father, who has set a restlessness in our hearts and made us all seekers after that which we can never fully find. Keep us at tasks too hard for us, that we may be driven to Thee for strength."

And it came to pass that this actress was "enjoying" one of those years when every kind of trouble hit her. She came back after every blow, better and happier than before—but when she lost her television show on the same day that her husband left her, she did get a little annoyed. She said: "I know the Lord won't send me more trouble than I have the strength to bear, but I do wish He didn't have quite such a good opinion of me."

Marian Anderson always carries this prayer in her heart: "Teach us, dear God, to have compassion enough to realize that all men are created equal in Thine image. Help us to understand that man's ultimate happiness depends upon his desire to seek greater wisdom for living so that he may share it with all mankind."

But this famous singer is the first to tell you, that if you want it to come to pass, you must give the Big Agent a little help. One teenager told the star, "I'd give anything in the world if I could sing like that!"

To this Marian smiled and replied, "Would you give eight hours of practice a day?"

It was Albert Schweitzer who said, "It is not enough merely to exist. It is not enough to say, 'I'm earning enough to live and to support my family. I do my work well. I'm a good father. I'm a good husband. I'm a good churchman.'

"That's all very well. But you must do something more. Seek always to do some good, somewhere. Every man has to seek in his own way to make his own self more noble and to realize his own true worth.

"You must give some time to your fellow man. Even if it's a little thing, do something for those who have need of a man's help, something for which you get no pay but the privilege of doing it. For remember, you don't live in a world of your own. Your brothers are here too."

Dr. Schweitzer's message could easily be the credo of show business. Actors don't like to get up in the morning, but they'll stay up all night and all day if they can help some person they never even met get out of the cellar and into the sunshine where he belongs.

Sammy Davis, Jr., once canceled a ten-thousand-dollar engagement in Boston because he promised me that he would appear for a group of youngsters at an Actors Youth Fund benefit. Louis Armstrong left a birthday party in his honor to play his heart out for some kids at a public school in Harlem. Martha Raye gave up a million dollars' worth of contracts to go to Vietnam and help nurse some of our boys back to life. Kathy

Crosby, the wife of the great Bing, took a course in nursing so she could help others. She feels that service to others is service to God, and she gives medical and educational service to the poor Mexicans in a little town in California. Instead of living a life of luxury and idleness, Kathy, like Martha and Sammy and Hugh O'Brian, finds happiness and contentment in reaching out to help others.

Hugh O'Brian told me, "In 1958 I had the thrill of spending six days with Albert Schweitzer in Africa and I came away with a better understanding of his great philosophy—of reverence for life and man's moral obligation to man—and I decided to create my own thing—to do something. And I started this youth foundation where I can help kids find the positive side of life and love, and make them law-abiding, normal, responsible members of the community."

As president of the Actors Youth Fund, I send hundreds of performers into the jungles of New York, to teach the disadvantaged kids the crafts of show business. I found out a long time ago that kids who commit crimes don't do it for eating money—but to show off.

So, Sid De May, a former hoofer and now executive director of the Actors Youth Fund, and I corralled the greatest showoffs in the world, the people of show business, to teach them how to show off for good instead of evil—and it works!

All of us in the entertainment world, at one time or another, have helped pass the hat in a room called America for one cause or another. Jerry Lewis has raised many millions of dollars to fight muscular dystrophy. Steve Allen is working to help retarded children. Bob Hope has done hundreds of benefits for the USO and Fight For Sight. Virginia Graham is on the stump for cancer research. Danny Kaye is active with UNICEF around the world. Jack Benny has spearheaded many drives for the State of Israel. Ed Sullivan and his entertainment troops have dedicated themselves to the Heart Fund. It was Eddie Cantor who first started the March of Dimes and later followed by Earl Wilson and his band of minstrels like Gypsy Rose Lee and others who raised enough money and love to find a cure for polio.

S
C
L
C

Southern Christian Leadership Conference

Martin Luther King Jr., *President*　　　　　Ralph Abernathy, *Treasurer*　　　　　Wyatt Tee Walker, *Executive Assistant*

September 9, 1963

Mr. Joey Adams
551-5th Avenue
New York 17, New York

Dear Joey:

I decided today that no matter what came up, I was going to sit down and write you a line. As I sat waiting my turn to speak at the Lincoln Memorial the other day, many thoughts came to me of how that grand day had come to be. I dated it from Birmingham more than any other place because for us it represented such a significant turning point. I could not help but remember how you came forward and through AGVA made a cultural siege of Birmingham as we had made a nonviolent siege.

There are no words to thank you and all the wonderful entertainers who wrote another chapter to the sage of Birmingham. With all of the obstacles that we faced in putting on the show, somehow we managed anyway. Even when the stage collapsed, the "show must go on" spirit prevailed. Lesser men and women would have called it a day.

All of this is said to say simply, thank you, for all that you have done. As I looked across the vast sea of faces, I saw people from Birmingham out there somewhere. They had come a long way, geographically and otherwise, and you, Joey Adams, helped them take a giant step.

Faithfully yours,

Martin Luther King, Jr.

K/r

The Martin Luther King, Jr., Letter

All of them, besides thousands of performers you never heard of, are living by Albert Schweitzer's words;—"Seek always to do some good somewhere—For remember, you don't live in a world all your own. Your brothers are here too."

The most treasured possession I have is not made of silver or gold. It's a letter from the greatest prophet of our time, the apostle of nonviolence, Dr. Martin Luther King, Jr., of Atlanta, Georgia, who led the civil rights movement in America until his tragic death by an assassin's bullet in Memphis, Tennessee in April 1968.

As a Gandhian evangel of love, hope and brotherhood, Dr. King lived and died in the service of God and man and in the advancement of mankind's immemorial vision, "Let freedom ring."

It was my great friend Dr. King who taught me the true meaning of "and it came to pass . . ." but not to stay. As he put it, "We shall overcome."

In 1964 this much-loved Baptist minister won the Nobel Peace Prize. At age thirty-five, the youngest person ever to receive the award, Martin Luther King, Jr., was nominated by the Swedish parliament, "because he had succeeded in keeping his follwers to the principles of nonviolence."

For nearly fourteen years, as president and founder of the Southern Christian Leadership Conference, Dr. King pressed his nonviolent protest against racial discrimination from backwater Southern towns to Northern city slums, to the halls of Congress. Even when his brother's church was bombed, he vowed, "If my father—or brother—or friends—or family go violent—I will stay nonviolent—" which became the symbol of that freedom revolution to millions, black and white, around the Earth.

It all started when Dr. King asked me to take a troupe of minstrels to Birmingham to make a cultural and a love siege of the south. How could we refuse? Benefits are an actor's way of praying—or giving gratitude. And this was the most important benefit we ever did in our lives. I'll let the *Congressional Record* tell you the story:

Show Business and Civil Rights—Non-violence in Birmingham

EXTENSION OF REMARKS

OF

HON. JACOB K. JAVITS

OF NEW YORK

IN THE SENATE OF THE UNITED STATES

Tuesday, October 8, 1963

Mr. JAVITS. Mr. President, in August a very heartening, but little-publicized event took place in Birmingham, Ala., that city of so much violence and danger for those engaged in the civil rights movement.

On August 4 the American Guild of Variety Artists, under the determined leadership of Joey Adams, its president,

In the first aircraft with Joey Adams were his wife, Cindy, and stars, celebrities, newspapermen, Life and Saturday Evening Post and other photographers, disc jockeys and commentators of radio and TV stations, plus several hundred pounds of food and drink, donated to Mr. Adams and his "Salute to Freedom" riders by Max Asnas, Stage Delicatessen. The planes were paid by donations which Mr. Adams got from Northerners, including $500 from Radio City Music Hall, Maurice Uchital ($2,500); David Dubinsky of ILGWU ($500); Jacob Potofsky of the Hatmakers' Union, $250. Union official Harold Gibbons, $1,000, AGMA, $200, and International Building Trades, $200 plus many smaller individual contributions.

expenses for this 'Sale to Freedom in Birmingham.'".

Threatening calls and letters, promises of bombings, riots and physical injury all failed to deter the group or the show which went on 9 p.m. and lasted for 5 hours. Ku Klux-ers and white violence groups began to hold meetings.

Joey Adams had collected for his production Johnny Mathis, Nina Simone, comedian Al Bernie, writers James Baldwin and Harry Golden, Dick Merson, assistant director of News; Billy Taylor and Wm. B. Williams of WNEW; Paul Duke, magician; Billy Rowe, formerly New York City deputy police commissioner, now Joe Louis' partner, and Conrad Buckner, dancer, the Gamm Sisters, the held a highly successful nonsegregated variety show entitled "Salute to Freedom," the proceeds of which were used to help defray expenses of the great civil rights march which took place here in Washington on August 28. The story of the show, given by a large mixed cast of performers and attended by a mixed audience of 22,000, is an inspiring testimonial to human dignity, just as was the march which it helped to support.

I ask unanimous consent that an article on the show, in the August 10 issue of the weekly Show Business, be printed in the RECORD at this point in my remarks.

There being no objection, the article was ordered to be printed in the RECORD, as follows:

NEITHER HEAT, BOMBS, NOR BIRMINGHAM COPS SHALL STOP THE SHOW—IT MUST GO ON

(By Leo Shull)

Two invasion planes flew into Birmingham, Ala., Monday, August 5, and captured the city.

"They captured the right people, too," said Rev. Martin Luther King, "the Negroes and whites who are fighting to attach Birmingham and the whole South to the United States of America." Joey Adams, president of AGVA, had decided to integrate Birmingham for the entertainment industry.

The first plane of showpeople drafted by Adams had 76 aboard. "The Spirit of '76," said Joey, who had conceived, produced, and financed the show and was now the denmother and nursemaid to the apprehensive collection of talent. The second plane departed afterwards and had Ray Charles and his orchestra crewmen and staff. Mr. Charles and his manager, Milt Shaw, with Stan Seldenberg, had chartered and paid for this plane.

To dare say, and a Yankee at that, that an integrated show would be smuggled into Birmingham to encourage Negroes and whites to integrate into a black and white audience was like waving a red flag in front of a bull O'Connor—an intolerable insult.

The enemy camp decided to meet it with volleys of silence, from the mayor of the city, the police, political figures and the Birmingham press which never printed a stick of linotype before or after the event. Blackout.

The police and mayor had refused protection, because "this was the first integrated show and audience in the history of Birmingham," declared Rev. A. D. King, brother of Martin Luther, who had organized 500 volunteers to deal with the local problems and preparations, including ticket sales for the show.

Taxi drivers had refused to transport the show's cast and personnel. Reverend King then collected a caravan of 50 private-car volunteers. Hotels had refused lodgings; Adams got a motel, run by A. G. Gaston, former Negro undertaker and now owner of the motel, the local Negro bank and Negro Insurance company to provide lodgings. Restaurants refused service. Adams brought along his own food. The city theater and auditorium owners had refused a meeting hall.

Adams and King got a Negro college campus. There were no chairs. Adams issued a radio call via Negro diskjockey in Birmingham asking people to carry their own—on the night of the show, for 3 miles people could be seen walking to the campus, carrying their own chairs—they had also paid $5 per ticket to see the show.

There was no stage or lights.

"Build one, buy lights," said Adams, "I'm sending a check for the lumber, lights and electricians. And don't spend a cent of the ticket sales, keep it all to pay for the march to Washington, August 28, I'm paying all

Raelettes, Clyde McPhatter, the Shirelles, Dick Gregory, Magid Triplets, the Alabama Christian Movement Choir of 150, the whole orchestra of the Harlem Apollo Theater led by its conductor, Reuben Phillips. The Alabama musicians' union refused to permit Negro and white musicians to play on the same stage.

The cast and crew got off the plane, had lunch at the Gaston Motel, then went to a nearby hall and began rehearsals with the orchestras. Sid DeMaye, of AGVA, began co-ordinating the stage routine.

Meanwhile in New York and over press wires the story began to go out. The radio stations from the North began phoning in for progress reports. The newsmen and photographers—about 50—began work. So did Cleveland Robinson, chairman of the march on Washington committee, Clarence Jones, of the Ghandi Society.

On the campus, Dr. Lucius H. Pitts, president of Miles College, had mustered volunteer students and alumni to prepare an organization of ushers, service personnel; the carpenters and roofmakers, lighting men and technicians were working in the 98-degree heat—an unusually hot day.

Civilian defense guards had been gathered to take over the protection job that the police refused and had always given to all other public gatherings—and these Negro volunteers came with shotguns to protect the audience from Ku Kluxers who had paraded a few days earlier in protest against the show.

Makeshift floodlights had been set up to light the way for the ticket buyers and to show up any lurking hoodlums or invaders. There were no toilet or restroom facilities, no water, since the field was about a half mile from the college, and 5 miles from center of town.

Although the show was not scheduled till about 9, the audience began to come at noon. Adams had expected 5,000; more than 20,000 people bought tickets, and brought chairs.

71

Many white ticket agencies accepted tickets for sale, a new first.

The Negro people, who had reason to dislike whites, treated the "Salute to Freedom" members with generous welcome and affection. The response to the show at times was deafening, and great roars greeted many of the acts and the quips of Master of Ceremonies Adams, Rev. Martin Luther King, Joe Louis. Adams made a point of publicly embracing many Negro members of the local committees, a sight that would have caused instant arrest a few months ago. The Negroes watched with disbelief and amazement as Negroes and whites chattered, worked, and mingled on stage and at the Gaston Motel (which had been bombed a few months ago when they found that Martin Luther King was sleeping on the second floor. A wall of new bricks replaces the old shattered one). Some Negroes asked if they could walk on the street with white members of the show; never seen in Birmingham before.

NBC and other televisions companies had brought their cameras, as did many of the film newsreel companies.

White and Negroes sitting and eating together became the big photo catch for Negro photographers shooting for southern Negro newspapers and magazines. More than a dozen Negro diskjockeys journeyed to Miles College and were introduced on the stage. They had been broadcasting this coming event for weeks.

Said James Baldwin to the audience: "This is a living, visible view of the breakdown of a hundred years of slavery—it means that white man and black can work and live together. History is forcing people of Birmingham to stop victimizing each other."

The only member of the U.S. Government or any of the 50 States to acknowledge there was a new kind of integration drive, was New York's Senator JACOB JAVITS. He sent a telegram to Joey Adams saying: "Congratulations to all those participating in this significant variety show, my warmest praise goes out to you for this inspiring show which deserves the support of all America interested in freedom and human dignity. Birmingham is an appropriate site for this event. I think this will become the symbol of the breakthrough so long awaited, and tell the people present I will work to overcome the Senate filibuster to bring civil rights this year."

About 4 hours after the show began as Johnny Mathis began his song, the stage collapsed and 50 people were hurled down, some of them struck by the falling lumber. The whole field went dark. Electricians restored lights in about a half hour, the audience stayed, the show went on. One man with two broken legs, and the other wounded were taken to hospitals.

The noise of the crash made people think a bomb had gone off, some jumped, John Mathis dove for the floor. (This writer was thrown clear to the grass below.) One of the Magid Triplets was injured, but he did his turn later anyhow. Orchestra instruments were broken, they will be paid for from the $10,000 fund Joey Adams raised.

Upon the return trip, a warning came that a bomb was on one of the planes. It was searched, then all plane riders were halted at the airport gate and questioned, some searched for possible bomb or weapon. The Ray Charles plane flew off. Then the 76 on the second plane embarked. At 5 a.m. it took off. At 9 a.m. it landed at LaGuardia, New York City, U.S.A., August 6, 1963.

Show Business and Civil Rights in The Congressional Record

It was the greatest show ever put on—but for a moment I thought it was our last.

When the stage collapsed, it was like a bomb going off. All the lights and microphones went dead. Twenty-three thousand people, black and white, were on the verge of panic. The hundreds of entertainers, musicians, stage crews and newspaper people were frozen in their places. The guards had their guns ready. Martin Luther King took my hand and walked stage front and center and said in a loud clear voice—with no microphone and only the moon as a spotlight, "If we panic now, if we all don't stay calm and 'trust in the Lord with all thy might,' we will be defeating all that we have done—all of us together—to bring faith to one another.

"With this faith we will be able to move out of the dark —to a beautiful daybreak. With this faith we will be able to transform the jangling discords of our nation into a beautiful symphony of brotherhood. With this faith we will be able to transform dark yesterdays into bright tomorrows and speed up that day when 'every valley shall be exalted, and every mountain and hill shall be made low; and the crooked shall be made straight, and the rough places plain: And the glory of the Lord shall be revealed—and all flesh shall see it together. . . .' "

Suddenly, out of the darkness and the stillness came one voice, "We shall overcome." Now, another voice, "We shall overcome—Deep in my heart I do believe—we shall overcome." Then the Alabama Christian Movement Choir joined in—now Johnny Mathis and Dick Gregory and Joe Louis and Harry Golden and William B. Williams and voices from every part of the arena were singing out loud and clear. Twenty-three thousand hearts singing as one:

> We shall overcome
> We shall overcome
> We are not afraid
> The Lord will see us through.
> Deep in our hearts we do believe
> We shall overcome.

Chapter 7.

Jerry Lewis

Jerry Lewis found joy in a mixed marriage because, as he says, "In our two-faith family, nothing is taken away—if anything, love of God is twice as much."

Jerry and Patti play the God bit all the way. I know the Big Boss must dig his billing at the entrance to the Lewis home. On the front door are two symbols: a mezuzah and a cross, and above them are two mottoes: "Shalom" and "Love One Another."

The Lewises have six children—all boys—Gary, Ronnie, Chris, Anthony, Joseph and Scott. When Jerry married Patti he promised her the world—and he darn near gave it to her. Both religions are taught to the boys. "Often in the evening when I'm hearing the younger children's prayers," Patti told me, "Jerry will come and stand in the doorway. First the boys will say Jewish prayers and then Christian prayers. That's the secret, you see, you double your pleasure and double your faith —and double your love of God."

The children, to this day, still open their gifts as they light the Hannukah candles, but now they keep the candlestick in front of the portrait of the Blessed Virgin. Jerry says, "It helps to have a Jewish mother keeping an eye on my *shiksa* (Gentile) wife."

Patti is a Roman Catholic and her husband is a Jew. When people ask if such a marriage didn't take courage, she tells them, "No, only ignorance.

"You see, when Jerry and I met I had no idea he was a Jew. My parents were Italian immigrants, and so was everyone else I knew.

"I was singing in a theater near our home in Detroit and Jerry was on the same bill. One look at that mop of black hair, and, well, I just took it for granted that he was Italian, too.

"Nowadays, it's hard to remember the kind of superstitious terror our little old-country community felt for Jews. There was only one Jew in our neighborhood, the man who kept the corner grocery store. As a little girl I used to run past his open door, as though the Devil himself lurked inside.

"My religious education was lacking in every way. Papa was a coal miner who was away most of the time. Mama worked in a factory and had no time for abstract ideas. There was always St. Anthony, of course, for whom my mother felt a warm devotion. He was Mama's special saint, and she kept a little statue of him in our apartment. But aside from St. Anthony, there were only two religious certainties in my life: You went to mass on Sunday and you ran when you saw a Jew."

Into this garden of Gentiles came Joseph Levitch, the grandson of an orthodox rabbi. Moses wasn't so Jewish. But by the time she knew this about Jerry, it was too late to run. They had two dates and already Patti discovered that "Life without him wasn't worth living." One afternoon she found a pair of soap baby shoes on her dressing-room table in the theater. On the makeup mirror above it he had scrawled in lipstick, "Let's fill these." And they filled a lot of them. For a time there when Jerry came home every night he didn't ask, "What's new?"— he asked, "Who's new?"

"It never even crossed my mind to ask Jerry to change his religion," Patti told me, "and, of course, he never insisted that I change mine.

78

"Maybe my mother didn't teach me too much theology, but she did teach me the essentials of married life—to cook, wash, sew and to obey your husband. There was no question in Mama's mind that it was the man who was the boss in the family."

Come to think of it, I must look into this Catholic bit—it sounds fascinating.

Jerry and Patti were still in their teens when they were married under the *chuppah* in the Synagogue. Jerry's parents and two of his aunts were the witnesses, holding the four posts of the *chuppah*, a kind of canopy under which the bride and groom stand. Patti was in a complete daze with the long Hebrew service. Above them the canopy sagged and drooped, as did the witnesses. She remembers only that Jerry nudged her, she said, "I do," and a wine cup was passed to both of them. They drank from it, to symbolize drinking together from the cup of life.

"For me now began the realization of something so unexpected," said Patti, "and yet so obvious, that I wonder how I could not have known it. Jews were as frightened of Christians as we were of them! I began to realize how deeply Jerry's family mistrusted the *shiksa*, the Gentile girl, in their midst.

"Probably the roughest time for me was when our first boy, Gary, was born. We were living in New Jersey, too far for my family to come, and that week Jerry had a much-needed job at a theater in Baltimore. He did get up to the hospital for the *bris*, the circumcision ceremony. In fact, his whole family turned out for it, for the birth of a boy in a Jewish family is a great event. But when the day came for me to go home from the hospital, although they knew Jerry was in Baltimore, not one of my new family appeared. I called a taxi to take me home, feeling as lonely—as lonely as the old Jewish grocer in Detroit must have felt when his Christian neighbors froze him out of their lives.

"The one in Jerry's family whose disapproval I feared most was his grandfather, the Rabbi. This tiny, beautiful old man was the last of a line of Rabbis going back many generations. Jerry's father, and now Jerry, too, had broken the tradition by going into show business. But one of the old man's daughters still kept a kosher home for him with two sets of dishes and strict rules for every phase of life. From sundown on Friday until sundown on Saturday he would carry no money, nor ride in any kind of vehicle. Saturday he would pray in the synagogue all day.

"Jerry adored him, and so,—shyly, not daring to say so— did I. I used to gaze at the wrinkled face between the skullcap and the beard, and think he was the saintliest man I had ever seen. I lived in terror that he would find me out. They had never dared tell him that his favorite grandson had married a Gentile, so I had been presented to him as a good Jewish girl, and coached before each visit as to what to do.

"One day when Gary was still a baby, we were visiting his grandfather in his little apartment in Brooklyn. Other relatives were there, too. Suddenly, Grandfather slapped the arm of his chair. 'You think you're fooling me—don't you?' he said, glaring around around at the roomful of children and grandchildren. He pointed a finger at me. 'I know she's a *shiksa*. I've known it from the first day.'

"I held my breath. The finger moved to Jerry. 'Now look at my grandson. She loves him. She takes care of him. He is happy. All this'—with a sweep of his arm he seemed to demolish candlesticks, prayer shawl, dietary vessels, 'all this is small before God. Love like theirs is big.'

"As the old man spoke, something small dropped from my eyes too. Behind the *chuppah* and *bris* I caught a glimpse of the God Jews worship, and He was the God St. Anthony worshiped too.

"My own first glimpse of the truth which was bigger than our differences came from his grandfather; Jerry's came through my mother.

"Mama had tried to be shocked about our marriage, but Jerry would always get her laughing and before long she loved him too. Still, she never stopped praying that I would be a good wife to him and a good Catholic. She gave me the little statue of St. Anthony to take with me into my new home.

"We'd been married ten years when Mama died. I'd gone

80

to mass, of course, all those years, and occasionally I'd ask Jerry just to step into the church with me to see that there was nothing to fear. But something always held him back.

"Loving Mama as he did, however, I was sure he would go with me to her funeral. And so he did. I don't know for whom I prayed harder that day, Mama or Jerry—that some hurt deep inside him would be healed, as it had been for me in his grand-father's home so many years before.

"I had my answer as we reached the sidewalk. 'I,' he said slowly, 'have been three times a blind, bigoted fool. Did you hear them talking about the children of Israel? Did you hear that about the son of David and Jerusalem? And they have candles, and vestments, and psalms—like in a temple!' "

That was the beginning of the end of all prejudices in the Lewis household. After that Jerry and Patti tried to outdo each other in appreciating each other's faith. Patti bought a child's book of Jewish history and read it aloud in the evenings. She got a Hebrew dictionary and she and the boys would surprise Jerry at the dinner table with the new words they learned. But Jerry topped them all with a single punchline:

"I believe," he said to Patti one day, "it would make you happy to have the children baptized."

Happy? It was the happiest day of her life. Jerry loved it, too, though he pretended great terror of the holy water and kept warning the priest not to get any of it on him by mistake.

To this day Jerry plays the game all the way, even though he acts like he's not enjoying it. "What do you do when your kids make with the communion bit?" I asked him. "Do you go to church with them and pray?"

"Sure," he answered, "but I only get down on one knee —that's for the Catholics. The other is for the Jews."

When Patti surprised Jerry with a large marble statue of Moses that she set up in their garden, Jerry matched her with a beautiful statue of St. Anthony that he stood beside Moses.

But even now Jerry makes a mock show of indignation at every Christian innovation. If Patti makes a sign of the cross at the table, he'll retaliate with an elaborate gesture that he claims is the Star of David. He keeps a jealous eye on Moses,

81

too, to be sure his flower bed gets as much attention as St. Anthony's. "Don't lose him in the bulrushes," he cries when the weeds get high.

Patti smiles at it all. "The fact is," she says, "that both of our faiths have been strengthened by knowing and loving the other one. Jerry's joy and pride in being a Jew, his love of his own traditions, his unceasing work for Israel—all of it has a new dimension now that he sees the place of all these things not only in his tradition but in mine. As for me, I know I am a better Christian after twenty-nine years of marriage to Jerry than I could ever have been by growing only in my own faith."

Those two beautiful people, Moses and St. Anthony must be getting their kicks as they dig the scene while watching over the Lewis's household.

After all, it was Moses who commanded everyone to honor their fathers and mothers and not to covet and/or mess around with their neighbors' wives. In other words, love what you have—and Jesus, St. Anthony's boss said, "This is my commandment, that ye love one another as I have loved you!"

Moses and St. Anthony came from two different books in the Bible but as they stand side by side now, holding court in the garden of the Lewis home, they must be very happy.

82

Chapter 8.

Gratitude

I was in South Vietnam during the war. You almost never think of anyone ever being in South Vietnam when there wasn't war. I was heading a troupe of minstrels to the troubled areas of the world for the President of the United States.

President John F. Kennedy had informed me that we were blazing a new trail. This was to be democracy in action. As President of the American Guild of Variety Artists and as a working comedian and master of ceremonies, he figured I was the logical one to head the United States' first cultural invasion of Southeast Asia and the underdeveloped areas of the world.

We were going to Kabul, Afghanistan, a split week in Katmandu, Nepal and Phnom Penh, Cambodia. Followed by one-night stands in Chiengmai, Udorn, Hua Hin, Lopburi, Karat and some of the smaller towns. I've heard of playing the sticks, but this was off-Broadway even to the Asians. Then on to Indonesia, India, Iran, Hong Kong, Singapore, downtown Bangkok and uptown Abadan.

This is no new gimmick to show people. Ever since young David played his harp to soothe King Saul, through the era of the court jesters to the age of the wandering minstrels and on to the era of two-a-day at the Palace, variety entertainers have been called upon to ease the tensions of a troubled world.

I was all for the idea when President Kennedy decided I would be his ambassador in greasepaint. I figured if we could make them laugh, how could they hate us? And if they applaud, how could they turn us away? I knew if they enjoyed our music, we must find harmony. I knew we couldn't lose if we pitted our jazz musicians against the martial music of the dictators surrounding them.

My band of minstrels—as disparate a lot of total strangers as ever stepped on a stage—numbered a pantomime comedian, a female magician, a jazz combo, three beautiful singing sisters, four black dancers, a couple of novelty acts and assorted extras of every size, color and talent.

For six months my soldiers in striped pants worked, toured and endured hardships, deprivations, little sleep, lots of bugs, heat, lousy conditions, audiences that didn't speak English, constant travel, new places, new customs, and new troubles daily. So, while we were saving the world, my minstrels were killing each other.

Feudin', fussin' and fightin' eventually became the cohesive cement among them. It degenerated to where the bickering was the only constant. The aggravation worked through to my Cindy who couldn't seem to shake it and could get no respite from the discord. Even when she was alone she would hear the arguments and talk to herself and think out what she should tell them if they start again.

As the deafening noises of anger and bitterness increased around her and within her, she lost the hearing in one ear. As her wall of resentment grew, another wall deep within her also grew. The other ear became blocked.

Cindy has long been a student of metaphysics and when things get thick around her it is her habit to turn to the Bible. She turned to the passage in Philippians 4:8. "Finally, brethren, whatsoever things are true, whatsoever things are honest, whatsoever things are just, whatsoever things are pure, whatsoever things are lovely, whatsoever things are of good report;

if there be any virtue, and if there be any praise, think on these things."

She tried to reverse the negative thinking and replace it with some good thoughts she could entertain about each person in each instance but the going was rough.

It was suggested that she see a doctor, that there are drops or treatments which help. Someone even mentioned an operation which cuts a window in the eardrum, but her years of training convinced her that you can't just handle the effects of the condition. What must be handled is the cause of the condition. You have to reach underneath to turn off the faucet producing the condition or its effects will spring up elsewhere—in an itch, a pain or some other seemingly causeless problem. Wholeheartedly she turned to God, her only physician.

When you're out of tune nothing seems to go right. The guy you need to reach just stepped out when you call, the plane you absolutely must make is full, the taxi situation is zero, just as it starts to rain. Conversely, when you're "in tune," what unfolds is a string of "coincidences." Coincidence, my wife has explained to me, is merely the spiritual agreement between God and man.

By "coincidence," she heard of an experienced metaphysician who was in Saigon temporarily. By coincidence (otherwise known as God's hand that was leading her) she met people who could take her to this lady. By coincidence the lady spoke a little English. Her diagnosis was so simple it was profound. . . . "Don't hear people; hear God." Listen for His word. Tune in to His thinking. Plug into His view of the whole situation. Open up to the fact that man is made in His image and likeness and is, therefore, contrary to physical sense testimony, spiritual and loving, harmonious and free.

Cindy slammed the door of her thinking shut on any further friction. She no longer allowed it into her thought. She substituted joy for frustration, harmony for inharmony, understanding for resentment and as she listened hard for God she began, bit by bit, to hear all the sounds of His universe. In a matter of time her hearing was perfectly restored.

Cindy's first gesture was to express her gratitude to God.

"How can I ever thank Him enough for the opportunity to serve my country and my God," she said. "But tell me, what good did we really do?" When I got back to Washington, the President and the Congress asked me the same question.

What good did we do? I've thought about that a million times. How do you put your finger on love? How do you put friendship down in a diary of events? How do you chronicle joy? How do you weigh warmth? How do you put a little orphan's smile into a letter to a congressman? How do you wrap up tears of gratitude from a wounded soldier and send it to the State Department.

"You want to know what good we did?" I said to Cindy. "I'll tell you what good we did. Remember the little baby whom we loved in the hospital in Singapore? Remember Lalida, age four? Remember how she hugged us and clung to us with all her might? Well, someday she'll grow up. And maybe someday she'll be in a position to return the friendship of an American who cared."

I told President Kennedy, as well as the Congress: "There are hundreds of thousands of Lalidas from four to twenty-four who, I'm sure, will always remember the bunch of Americans who went out of their way to bring them joy. And these youngsters could be tomorrow's leaders, in business, in government. Perhaps, in the coming generation, when these children will be making the decisions for their country, they'll think more kindly of Americans because of the Americans who thought kindly of them.

"You want to know what good we did? I'll tell you what good we did. Remember all those thousands of soldiers we worked to in the up-country jungles of Thailand? And the wounded veterans whom we visited, ward by ward, in the hospital in Saigon? And the Lao army we entertained in Vientiane? And the thousands of young men who sat cross-legged on the ground in Afghanistan? And the fighting Nepali Gurkhas who filled our outdoor stadium in Katmandu that afternoon? And those blocks and blocks of refugees from Red China? Remember them?

"Well, they'll remember us, too. And if the time ever comes that any of those men will be asked to point a gun in the direction of an American, maybe they'll think twice. Maybe they'll remember that they might be shooting at a little comic in baggy pants that made them laugh. Or a thin, shy, little clarinet player with glasses, who held a jam session for them on the steps of a temple or the balloon man who fashioned toy animals for them and their children. Maybe they'll remember that we are their friends. That's the good we did.

"You want to know what good we did?" I said again. "I'll tell you what good we did. We showed these countries that Americans are human beings just like they are. That we laugh and fight and eat and cry just like they do. That we have problems just like they have. That we can share a rice bowl with them, that we're sensitive to their customs and can join in the Thai dancing of Thailand and can enjoy the Bharatana-tyam dancing of India.

"We lived with them, walked with them and talked with them. They saw one of us unhappy because we didn't get a letter from home; they saw one of us with a belly-ache; they saw another of us thrilled because we were getting the cloth their country was famous for or the stones their country was proud of and were able to send it home to a loved one.

"No more will we be just a faceless mass of wealth and power and atom bombs—or even a number in a ledger to these people. Perhaps some of them know us as flesh and blood people just like they are and not as the militaristic, imperialistic aggressors we're made out to be. Maybe, America will be a singer with soft, brown hair whom they heard in church one morning, or a comedian with a straw hat whose hand they shook one afternoon, or a black dancer who showed them that we know the meaning of brotherhood. That's the good we did."

Talking about ambassadors in greasepaint, I'd like you to meet the Ambassador of Love—*Pearl Bailey*. This Presidential appointment was ratified by all of us in show business:

Greetings:

Reposing special trust and confidence in your integrity, prudence, and ability, I hereby appoint you Ambassador of Love to the entire world, authorizing you hereby to do and perform all such matters and things as to the said place or office do appertain or as may be duly given you in charge hereafter.

Richard M. Nixon

Pearlie Mae is also a pretty good ambassador for the Almighty. Just listen to her prayer for the beginning of each day:

"Dear God, please take your fingertips and lift the corners of my mouth at the beginning of each day. Let me smile when the fire of humanity starts to burn hot and would melt your perfect mold. Kindle your fire of love and harden the corners so they cannot drop to scowl."

I fell in love with Pearl Bailey on her fiftieth birthday. It happened when the March of Dimes honored her for her work for all charitable causes and I was the Roastmaster. Every year show business honors one of its own, and in the tradition of our craft, we roast the one we love. The idea is, "if you can't say anything nice about the guy, let's hear it." I have murdered everybody from Ed Sullivan (You can sum up his career in one word—lucky) to Johnny Carson (Success hasn't changed him— he's still the same arrogant bum he always was) to Jack Benny (He's always sitting with his back toward the check) to Jerry Lewis (He's a modest fellow—and he has a lot to be modest about).

Of course, I often have the help of such pallbearers as Bob Hope, Milton Berle, Georgie Jessel, Don Rickles and other killers.

On the night we honored Pearl Bailey, the dais was loaded with stars ready to hit their target for charity. "I just can't do it," I said to Pearlie Mae. "It's not easy roasting you. You're a lady, you're fifty, you're black and I'm white, I just can't . . ."

"If you spare the rod," she cracked, "I'll never forgive you. If I can dish it out, I can take it—and I want to be treated like one of the boys." Although she really couldn't fit into their clothes too well, I said okay.

It was tough. But how can you refuse such an invitation? "Pearl Bailey," I started, "has just had her mouth declared a lethal weapon." Milton Berle said, "If she becomes Jewish, I'll make her a star—then she and Sammy Davis, Jr., can open their own synagogue." Georgie Jessel said, "They are testing her to play the old Mae West parts—the only trouble is, her old parts don't work as good as Mae West's did." Don Rickles cracked, "Pearl got a call from God—collect—she is really Billy Graham in pantyhose."

Pearlie Mae laughed the loudest at all the jibes. When our Ambassador of Love responded, it was full of gratitude—gratitude for the friends who liked her enough to roast her, gratitude for her chance to help the March of Dimes, and gratitude to God for making it all possible.

The punchline in one of the hymns is, "Gratitude is riches —complaint is poverty." In that case, Pearlie Mae is the richest lady I know.

Of course, our gal wasn't handed it all on a silver stage. She has always made it the hard way—but always the church and prayer were part of it. "As a little girl I remember my father preaching at the House of Prayer," Pearlie reminisces, "Those members really shouted and they got so happy they fell under the power and jumped up and down and when the older folks shouted and jumped, their money would fall out of their pockets—and that was the cue for the children. We got extremely happy too and started to shout and fell under the power but on top of the money. While I was on the floor I used to hear people say, 'Look at Elder Bailey's girl so happy—isn't that wonderful.' Brother, I had to stay down there for financial gain —I hope I'm forgiven for that sin."

Pearlie Mae has been a fighter all her life. She has had to fight poverty, sickness, bigotry, hate, but the answer was always love. When she entered the hospital in 1965 she was really down. She felt she was going no place and she had so much to give. She prayed for guidance—only so that she could help others. It was the doctor who was sent as the guardian

91

angel. "You're somebody special," he said. "You must take care of yourself. God puts His finger on some, but He has put His whole hand on you."

"That did something to me," says Pearl. "Ever since that day I have felt more optimism and love. Since then I have known that I must use my right to give and receive love. I know that man can take nothing from me. He can neither give breath, nor take it away. I have come to think of myself as somebody with something to give. How nice . . . I shall bestow it as given: Man, take it or leave it. How man receives my love is his concern. I shall just give in love."

That's exactly what our Ambassador of Love does, too. Did you ever notice that in all her shows since that day at the hospital, she encourages people to come to the stage and touch her—shake her hand—make contact. "I feel a great healing power," she says, "so when they run up to the stage and we touch, I am healed and so are they. The sickness of hatred and confusion disappears and we all are free."

Pearl and I have sat around talking our hearts out many a night. Pearl says she is neither a pessimist nor an optimist. "I'm a realist."

"That's it," I said. "What men usually ask of God when they pray is that two and two not make four."

"True," Pearlie Mae said. "The trouble is we have just enough religion to make us hate—but not enough to make us love one another."

I actually heard one man praying, "Oh, God, help our side, and if you can't, at least don't help them other bums."

"Sometimes," Pearl remarked, "a nation abolishes God— but fortunately God is more tolerant.

"The big answer is gratitude and faith. Many people get to a detour in the road and think that's the end of the road entirely. That's when they give it all up. I just want to remind you—there's an arrow there. It shows you where the detour goes. All you have to do is look for it, and if you follow it, you will eventually get back on your course. Going a bit out of your way shouldn't bother you. Sometimes it's even necessary to back up. The big thing is the faith that you will make it eventually. The alternative is plunging off the bridge that isn't there."

Pearl has been in and out of hospitals for years, but with each experience comes a better understanding and even more joy. One night she received a revelation. It was when she was at her lowest and she was praying "for true deliverance unto God." She found herself writing down a prayer. "I hope you take these words to your hearts and keep them warm with love," she says. "I was praying for you, too, friends."

Dear God, speak to me tonight, give me a little more wisdom, more knowledge, more love and understanding for my fellow man. Cleanse me of all my misgivings and set me straight on the path. Direct my feet to the places where I can speak of You with great reverence. Open ears so they can hear of the great things that are here for us. Let us awaken to all the beauties of the earth, let the peace that passes all understanding reach out now to all mankind. We are in trouble, we are confused, we are bitter, going down deeper into the mire. Throw us a branch strong enough to pull us out. Our feet are stuck in clay of hate, deceit, and malice. Soften the earth where we stand so we can loosen ourselves, teach us to smile again. Let me walk with and for Your cause alone, alone. Oh, God, I am listening every day. What is this thing I must do? If I'm not ready, speak directions in my ears, guide my feet, quicken my thoughts. Prepare me, dear Lord, prepare me. Help us to learn to help ourselves. We stand in our corners waiting for You. You are there—You are here. Let us join with You.

Gratitude is riches. Complaint is poverty. Joan Fontaine was sitting next to me at the opening of a new show. "Wow," I said, "you look prettier and younger than ever. What's the answer, Joan?" "Gratitude," she said, "instead of complaining about what's wrong, I am grateful every moment for what's right."

That's the whole idea: We are quick enough to complain and run to God when we are displeased with something—but

93

are we grateful enough when God has been good to us? God wants to hear a word of praise, too. After all, He made it all possible.

Like the little girl who was saying her prayers. She asked for all kinds of goodies—from toys to special foods. She took care of her mother and dad and all her playmates. Now she looked up and said, "Okay, now, God, is there anything I can do for you?"

Thinking good is thanking God. And gratitude is a way of living. Gratitude makes you eager to reciprocate. When we realize that our success and happiness is due to the loyalty, helpfulness and encouragement we have received, our desire grows to pass on similar gifts to others. Gratitude spurs us on to prove ourselves worthy of what others have done for us. Gratitude is a way of worship.

Don't take my word for it. I'm only repeating what happy people are saying. All through the Psalms the emphasis is on thankfulness. "Sing to the Lord with thanksgiving," "O, give thanks unto the Lord, for He is good; for His steadfast love endures forever."

A thankful heart is the key that opens our lives to the goodness of God.

Claudia McNeil is a good example.

"God gives us so much," she says, "and so many blessings and we never give Him anything. The least we can do is give Him gratitude. Through things I learned on my own and through my mother, I figured out He gives us our own free will and within that we have to choose what we please; bad or good. Well, I gave Him back my free will and let Him run my life as He sees fit. I follow His footsteps. I walk in His way, not Him in my way, which I find has given me a happier and easier life. When I don't understand what His answers are to my prayers, whether the answer is yes or no, I ask Him to lead me as a child and this is the way I go. I talk to God as a friend with depth.

"When I met one of the high officials of the Vatican, he said, 'You know, Claudia, I think God gets a little tired of formal prayers all the time.' Even when I'm walking down Fifth Avenue I talk to Him in my mind. Before every show I kneel down and dedicate my show to God. Because I'm so happy in my profession, I feel selfish, so I just donate my shows to God."

It's okay to ask God for help. He is the first to listen and do something about it, but you've got to give Him a little cooperation, too. You can't lie in bed and ask for favors and then wait there until it comes to you. You've got to get out of bed and go to work.

I must tell you this story. Well, I don't exactly must, but it proves a point—and if it doesn't, forget I mentioned it!

This actor hadn't worked in years. He was waiting for a call from his agent. He was too big to go to auditions or even try out for parts. He just stayed in bed and prayed. "Please," he begged of God, "you know me. I'm always praying to you and yet I have nothing but bad luck, misery, sickness and no good parts in years—and look at Richard Burton—he's never prayed in his life, and yet he is always working. He's rich, he's successful. How come a believer like me is always in trouble and he is always doing good?"

Suddenly a big booming voice sounded in his ear. "Because Richard Burton isn't always bugging me—that's why."

James Brolin, who plays Dr. Steve Kiley on TV's "Marcus Welby, M.D.," could have been his own patient recently. The old car he was driving turned over, throwing him out of it. Then the car came to rest, with one of the wheels on top of his hand.

"I thought it was all over," Brolin says, "and then I started to pray. As it turned out it could have been a lot worse. Sure, my hand was broken. But I was grateful—so grateful—to be saved. I attribute my survival to Divine Power."

There goes that word gratitude again. It's what makes the world go round. "Because of my faith in the Man Upstairs," Jimmy says, "and then in myself, I'm where I'm at today. And I can honestly say that my faith in God saved my life, and in more ways than one. My belief in God has helped me form lasting values for my life and channel my energies into something I think is contructive."

Mahalia Jackson was America's great gospel singer. For forty years or more she made "a joyful noise unto the Lord." Born into an indigent Negro family, she left school at age twelve to work full-time in the Louisiana cotton fields, then to factories in Chicago, scrubbing floors along the way, and on to Carnegie Hall, London's Albert Hall and stardom all over the world.

"God can make you anything you want," Mahalia told me. "He can lift you up—but you have to put everything into His hands."

Gratitude is what made Mahalia Jackson reach out to help others. She loved to appear at an Actors Youth Fund show so she could show her gratitude to God for all the good He gave her.

"I'd like to tell everyone that God's got the whole world in His hands," she told the youngsters. "I'd like to tell everyone that God can take nothing and make something of it. If I have accomplished anything, it is nothing but the grace of God that has brought me this far. God has sent me all over the world just singing the simple songs of the South. That's why I love to sing, 'He's Got the Whole World In His Hands.' "

Mahalia dedicated herself to the youth. It was her way of sharing her gratitude: "I want to prove to young people that they can take what they've got and go to great heights if they believe in themselves and have faith in God. I say to them, 'The Lord took me, and I was nothing, and He put me up. It can happen to you too. If the Lord can bring me this far—take me out of the washtubs and off my knees scrubbing other peoples' floors—then He can do as much and more for others.' "

Chapter 9.

Sammy Davis, Jr.

Sammy Davis was on the golf course with President Nixon and was asked what his handicap was. "Are you kidding?" he quipped. "I have one eye, I'm black and I'm Jewish—any other silly questions?"

Sammy has had to have a sense of humor to survive all three. When he first converted to Judaism, he met Milton Berle and bragged about it.

"Fine," said Milton, "but you just blew the New York Athletic Club."

Our hero loves to joke about his background: "My mother is Puerto Rican, my father is colored, my ex-wife is Swedish, and I'm Jewish—man, there ain't too many neighborhoods I can move into."

But when he gets serious, he hits like a heavyweight. "If I ever need a heart transplant," he likes to say, "I hope they give me the heart of a bigot or a racist—because it's never been used."

One time he had a heckler in the audience who evidently was colorblind. Sammy bopped him on the head with his funnybone. "If you're ever in California, sir, I do hope you'll come to my house and use my pool—I'd like to give you some drowning lessons."

Sammy brings home his point by the story he tells about getting on a bus in the south and was told by the bigoted driver to go sit in the back. "But I'm Jewish," Sammy protested.

"Get off altogether," shouted the driver.

Nobody works harder, plays harder, laughs harder or cries harder than Sammy Davis, Jr. I saw him sob his heart out when his friend Martin Luther King died. I saw him laugh hysterically when he was embraced by President Richard M. Nixon. I watched him perform at hundreds of charity drives, often when he was too sick and too tired to go on. I saw him give up a paid job to do a benefit for the Actors Youth Fund because he didn't want to let a bunch of kids down.

Not long ago, Sammy and I had a very busy day playing the benefit circuit. In one afternoon we performed at a Catholic church, a Protestant church and a Jewish temple. After a tired, but happy tour, Sammy embraced me and said, "We should be proud this day. We just played God across the board.

"And," says Sammy, "nobody prayed harder than I when I thought I was going to be blind."

Sammy can laugh at it now. But he recalled: "Until I lost my eye in that automobile accident, I never gave God much thought at all. I mean I believed in Him, but I've got to admit that religion was never uppermost in my mind. But I got a picture of myself out on that highway that would have scared an atheist into church. It was the most desperate floating-in-space kind of helplessness I ever knew. That's when I begged God not to let me go blind.

"Here I was turning to Him and I had no right to even hope He was listening."

But you can bet your last buck that God is always on the alert for anybody that turns to Him. Sammy soon realized that God will be close to anybody who will let Him. Didn't he send a guardian angel to the hospital in the person of Eddie Cantor to talk to him and give him hope and love and faith?

"Sammy," Eddie said, "you've got a tough fight ahead of you, but you've also got great strength. Never forget what an

100

enormous gift God gave you when he gave you your talent. Treat it as you would everything precious and rare. Protect it, use it well and it will carry you wherever you want to go—and God is a gracious giver. He'll take you all the way.

"Remember—God put you on this earth to glorify Him."

It's just what Sammy needed to turn him on. Later he let his heart down to his rabbi: "On the one hand, God gave me talent. Why me instead of some other guy? Very few black men have been given the chance to see what I've seen, do what I've done and go where I've gone. Why was I given this pass to a good life? Now, on the other hand, He puts me in an accident. When I felt the crash, I figured it was all over for me. Then I woke up and I wasn't exactly better off, but I was in fairly good shape. So, I started thinking, why did he put me in this accident and then save me?

"I kept thinking—maybe He's trying to tell me something. Did I do something wrong? Did I let Him down somewhere along the line?"

"Sammy," the rabbi explained, "I can only interpret your experience according to our philosophy. We don't believe that goodness should stem from threat of punishment. We worship God in love, not in fear. It is written: 'Whom the Lord loveth, the Lord correcteth. Therefore, should a man see suffering come upon him, let him scrutinize his actions.' We believe a warning such as yours comes not to punish for wrongs, but to shake you up a little and perhaps stimulate some spiritual progress. Exactly the kind of thinking you are doing now. You're wondering what you might have done wrong. Turn it slightly. Have you done as much as you might have with what God gave you to work with?"

Every time I saw Sammy after that, playing God across the board, I knew he could honestly say, "Yes."

It's Red Skelton who said about our Sammy, "He wears the Star of Davis around his neck."

Chapter 10.

Thy Will Be Done

Butterflies Are Free was inspired by Harold Krents, the handsome, young, blind lawyer from Washington, D.C.

He lost the sight of one eye when he was nine years old, and shortly after that he became totally blind. "I had one of three choices to accept," Harold told me. "Either God is dead —or God has a distorted sense of humor—or there must be a reason. We are all his children, and he has a plan for us. I chose the last one."

Harold says, "God has been good to me. I'm sighted—I just can't see. But my problem tends to make me stronger. It gives me a real sense of determination. You can't have the luxury of squandering the abilities you have.

"God's will be done. Because of my being blind, I was able to develop a photographic memory—which certainly comes in handy to a lawyer."

Krents's book, *To Race the Wind,* is full of hope and joy. "Life is a challenging experience," he says. "Who knows where we're going? You can walk across the street and get hit by a Volkswagen and how will your sight help you then? You've got to make good with what you've got—and make it real good."

Harold decided a long time ago that the key to life is to find humor in everything you do. "I'm sure if I could see Him, God is wearing a great big grin. Because I am blind, I can see Him better now."

The Harold Krents story proves the rule for show people. I don't know a star worth his billing who hasn't come up off the canvas a hundred times or more before he hit the big time. And they can take it even if God is dishing it out—because they know He has a better plan for them just around the corner—if they believe.

Like the little six-year-old show kid who was saying his prayers, "Please, God, make my Mommy a hit in the show tonight and please take care of Daddy and my little brother, Tom, and Grandpa and Grandma and please, God, take care of yourself, because if anything happens to You, we're all sunk."

Contrary to the concept of Broadway and Hollywood as twin capitals of the tinsel world of sin, many of the leading citizens are devout believers. St. Patrick's and St. Malachy's, St. Bartholomew's and St. Thomas's, Temple Emanu-El and the Actors' Temple are pretty good attractions for the theater mob, especially when a show is opening or the critics weren't too good.

Most of them rarely miss a mass or a holiday. It is not uncommon to see a star on the eve of his or her opening go to church to pray—armed with a run-of-the-play candle.

Almost every one of these stars has had to overcome a kick in the heart at one time or another, but they are ready to accept God's will and go on to bigger and better things. That's what makes them stars.

Carl Erbe, the dean of the Broadway press agents, does all his business in New York. But he can't move from his Long Island home because his dog is blind and is comfortable roaming around the old house and knows where to find everything.

Some years ago when Mary Pickford learned that her ex-mother-in-law was desperately ill, she went to visit the elderly lady. Miss Pickford told the patient, "I don't know if you remember, but I'm a Christian Scientist. And if you have a Bible here, I'd like to read something to you." Mrs. Moore, a devout Catholic, replied, "Mary dear, all I'd ask of Christian Science is that it get me up in time for mass."

One star came into New York after a disastrous trip on the road. The critics and the public slaughtered his show but you just couldn't stop him. Right before the curtain on opening night he prayed to the Head Critic, "Oh, Lord, if it be possible, please justify our opinion of ourselves."

Barbara Berjer, the star of "The Guiding Light," says, "I couldn't live without my faith." The mother of a son handicapped by cerebral palsy, Barbara has leaned heavily on her faith to take her through this storm. She and her husband and their son, now in his twenties, attend the Church of Religious Science regularly and work with God all the time.

"Religion is one of the strengths which have helped me to overcome tragedy," Barbara says. "Nobody is given problems they don't have the capacity to handle. We're different people because of this challenge. We knew from the beginning that this was the problem and we applied ourselves and are richer people because of what's happened to us."

TV host Mike Douglas is one of the best-liked of the show-business fraternity—especially lately. Mike drove himself all his life to become a star, living on a treadmill, sacrificing his family pleasures and his friends. It finally came when he was 35 years old. "From 19 to 35 is a lot of years of waiting," Mike says now. "That's a lot of food cooked in hotel rooms and a lot of pants pressed by my wife Gen in cramped backstages. It's a lot of maneuvering to keep our twin daughters and Gen and me together as a family."

If you ask Mike if it was all worth it, he will tell you that life as a TV star wasn't that rich. "It certainly wasn't that enjoyable or satisfying until I learned the greatest lesson of my life," Mike will tell you.

Ironically enough, it was the death of his brother Bob that made him a better man. "My older brother was a star in everything he did, and he was my hero. He was my special champion and protector. He was my teacher and my inspiration. He had the touch for making my dreams come true.

"When my big brother was taken to the hospital and I was told that he was dying, I was in a state of shock. I knew that this was my chance to reverse the roles. This was my opportunity to be Bob's champion and protector. But I was powerless. I had money and connections. I could give him the best now—but I was powerless.

"I don't recall exactly how it happened or what prompted me to do it, but sometime during that long night, walking the hospital floors, I began to pray. I knew little about prayer. It had never been like me to run to churches and light candles; church had always been Bob's department. He had always tried to make me think more seriously about religion, but I had resisted.

"I wasn't begging, I just wanted Bob to feel what I was feeling—the presence of God—and I wanted God to know what a fine man my big brother was and how grateful I was for Him. Isn't it odd, in the midst of approaching death, mine was a prayer of gratitude."

Bob died and Mike went back to his TV show in Philadelphia but no day since has passed that he doesn't say a prayer and thank God for his family and his health and his job. "I'm new at it," Mike says, "and I don't really understand all the ramifications of its power—but today I could not live without prayer.

"It's interesting that since I stopped running so hard and pushing so hard; ever since Bob died, people are telling me I look better. It's for sure I feel calmer. Now, before every show there's always time when I go off into a corner to say a very private prayer. Sometimes, then, I remember it was Bob, really, who taught me to pray. When this thought comes to me, I smile. You see, he's watching over his little brother still."

Virginia Graham overcame tragedy and death with love, faith and laughter.

She made medical history by licking what was diagnosed as terminal cancer—and gave hope and courage to thousands by proving it can be done. She laughs about it now. "One woman at a dinner introduced me as 'the lady who discovered cancer.' Another woman came up to her and said, 'I don't know one woman that cancer did so much for.'"

When her husband, who was always at her side, was in the hospital for a long stretch of mental illness, Virginia got him out with prayer and faith—and kept herself from joining him by laughing at it all. "How could any man in his right mind live with me all these years?"

What's great about my friend Virginia is that she can laugh at herself and even more important, make you laugh with her while you forget your own troubles.

"The secret of my endurance," quips the 'Girl Talk' star, "is that the thin girls watch me because they feel superior and the fat ones relate to me. I get them coming and going.

"Maybe," she says, "I'm the viewer's conscience. Actually, I'm very moral. I'm the Bible Belt of the network."

I think they go with her because she's the most honest lady on television. When she had a face lift, she broke all the rules describing it to her television audience. "I don't look younger," she admitted, "just healthier! The bags under my eyes are gone. So is my double chin. If I have one more face lift, there will be nothing left in my shoes." The men were horrified at her honesty, but the women thought it was terrific."

Virginia has proven to be a maverick all her life. "I was told I could never have children," she says. "I'd had a very serious operation before Lynn was born." But her daughter Lynn is living evidence not only that she could, but did.

"My family is my greatest reward," she says. "I feel like I was God's assistant in making it all come about. And I did it all with prayer and faith." Virginia says that she is one of the luckiest girls who ever lived. But it was never really a matter of only good luck, because she's had both kinds—the worst and the best. "I had typhoid when it wasn't popular, I've had three fires and half a dozen burglaries that wiped us out, they told me I wouldn't survive this cancer. I even wanted to end it all instead of a lingering death.

"In that moment of decision, I remembered what my father had said to me as a little girl. I had asked him, 'Where is God, Papa?' and he answered, 'Right in your heart.'

"My recovery began in that very moment of recollection, and I've been going up, up and away ever since. None of these catastrophes have left a single scar, but that's how God works —He takes you all the way."

Along with your faith comes the realization that all of us have the same Father—no matter what our individual differences may be. Dick Van Dyke tells the story of the girl who asked her seven-year-old schoolmate, "What church do you go to?"

"I don't go to church," her friend said. "I go to a temple. I'm a Jewess."

"What's that?" asked her questioner.

"You know there are Protestants, Catholics, and Jews," the girl explained. "But they are all just different ways of voting for God."

I have voted a straight ticket for God ever since I registered in kindergarten. Recently I went to Him for some patronage. I figured I had built up enough points to ask for a special favor.

I was opening at the Rainbow Grill atop Rockefeller Center with my own show. It was a very important engagement for me. All my friends made reservations, including Governor Nelson Rockefeller and Attorney General Louis Lefkowitz, who were going to introduce me. Ed Sullivan, Earl Wilson, Jack Dempsey and 250 other celebrities and critics were coming to see if there were still any snappy songs and fancy patter left in me.

The day before I opened, I came down and I do mean down, with a bad case of vertigo. It had been coming on for months, but now I was completely off-balance and couldn't walk without help. How could I make it to that stage alone? How could I do the dances, sing the songs? How could I stand up?

That's when I went to my Candidate for a favor. "Thy will be done," I pleaded. "But *now?*"

When the angel appeared I didn't even recognize her. She was a Bible student who was visiting with my Cindy and she just happened to have the medicine I needed. "Oh ye of little faith," she ad-libbed from the Good Book. "When Moses came to the Red Sea, with the Egyptians in hot pursuit, he asked the Jews to follow him. God said He would take them across in safety—their faith would take them all the way.

"First they went into the sea up to their ankles, then up to their knees, then up to their hips, their shoulders, their chins —and *then* the waters opened and they all went over in safety.

"Trust in the Lord with all thy heart and lean not to thy own understanding. In all thy ways acknowledge Him and He will direct thy path."

That was it for me. I knew then if I just went forward and trusted in the Candidate I voted for all my life, He would take me all the way, He would put the words in my mouth and the song on my lips—so I just kept coming and all the waters opened up. It was a wonderful opening night, and I never missed a show—twice a night, for the next three weeks—or my daily radio show—or the benefits.

The big thing to lick was fear. But when you realize that each individual is a distinct expression of God, possessed of His goodness, living in His harmonious realm, governed by His law, there is no room for fear or anguish. All you have to do is keep going and He will part the waters and direct thy path.

I know I sound like a big hero now. But the truth is I still get a little scared every once in a while. But at least now I know where to go. A dozen doctors weren't able to put me on my feet—but one message from the Lord not only put me on my feet, but kept me dancing all night.

The other day I felt ill and as usual, I complained to my wife. "Why me?" I cried. "What have I done to deserve it?"

"It's what you haven't done," she answered. "Have you thanked God lately for all the good you have? Did you thank Him for putting you on your feet? And keeping you there? And—"

"Giving me such a gorgeous wife to remind me," I added.

That's why I'm putting this down here—to show that I am grateful and to remind you to do the same. "All things work together for good for those who love the Lord."

Chapter 11.

Ethel Waters

The lady sitting opposite me at my WEVD microphone was black, beautiful and looked half her 76 years. "Wow, Ethel," I said, "you look gorgeous."

"Naturally," she laughed, "God is in the beauty business."

Only a few years before, Ethel Waters, fed up with the "Stormy Weather," was ready to give up. She was too fat, too poor, too sick and too tired to fight. As President of the American Guild of Variety Artists, I spoke to her about going into the AGVA Home for the Aged.

Now, as she talked to me, she was alive and gay and vibrant. "What a change," I exclaimed, "your voice is better than ever, you look so young and happy."

"Easy," she explained, "it's just that I was lazy. God has so many goodies for everybody and he puts them all in front of you. All you have to do is bend down and pick them up . . . and that's just what I did."

"But," I persisted, "the last time I saw you, Ethel, you weighed 350 pounds, you were sick, you had nothing to look forward to but despair, and now you're filled with the glories

115

of God and at 76 you're looking upward. I never saw you so happy."

"It's no big secret," she answered. "I've never been that far away from God that I can't reach him when I need Him. I just decided that I had to pick up our friendship again—and, boy, it's the greatest love affair of all time."

"Just like that?" I asked.

"Exactly," she said, "the Lord gave me fresh answers to my problems. For one thing, I realized that although I hadn't been displeasing Him too much, I hadn't been really pleasing Him either. Until I joined Billy Graham, I was never really happy or sure of myself. I was always doing some show or nightclub act; but this ain't no show, baby, and it ain't no act. I'm a born-again Christian, doing what I was always intended to do."

"I love getting up at the Billy Graham Crusades, making 'a joyful noise unto the Lord'—it shows that being a witness for the Lord is no hard, long-faced affair, but the easiest, gladdest thing that I or anybody ever did!"

The Ethel Waters story is filled with stormy weather. She was born out of wedlock, the daughter of a twelve-year-old black girl who had been raped at knifepoint. She grew up in the worst slums and back-alley neighborhoods with her frightened, unmarried, child-mother. Most of the time she had to steal in order to eat.

"The Lord is Almighty," Ethel says now. "But don't forget the Devil," she laughs. "He can be pretty powerful. I know because I used to be one of his best customers. Let me tell you, he lost a good bet when he lost me!"

Ethel has come a long way on faith. "It wasn't always easy," she admits. "I was one of the worst brats in my neighborhood. It doesn't matter now who knows that I was a ringleader of street gangs and street life in the slums. I only know that one night in church when I got up off my knees, it didn't matter no more that I'd been bad. It still doesn't matter. That's all gone because God and I are together again.

"No success, no stardom on stage, nightclubs or motion pictures, no big money or big awards, nothing ever measured

116

up to what I had lost with Jesus. I still believed in Him. I prayed. I read my Bible and cried out for help in my times of trouble—and, boy, I had plenty of it. I asked His help before every performance. But with all the bows I took, with all the cheers and raves, with all the fancy clothing and jewelry, riding around in those big cars, I still felt lonely for Jesus. Still missed the joy, the security, the peace of that shining, beautiful thing we'd once had—together."

Ethel has found it all as an evangelist. Spreading the word of God has added years to her life and taken off 200 pounds from her body. From the moment she started doing her thing with the Lord on the Billy Graham crusade, she knew it would be a hit. "How could it fail?" she asked. "You know God never sponsors a flop."

Ethel was radiant as she talked to me now. The lady who created such hits as "Dinah," "Am I Blue," "Stormy Weather," and starred in *As Thousands Cheer,* and dozens of other shows and pictures, would only talk about her contract with the Lord.

"But," I asked, "if you give up show business and stay strictly with the God bit, how are you going to get along?"

"Through the love and grace of God. Don't worry about Ethel. The Lord will take good care of me," she explained. "I sing strictly for Him now. My voice may be mostly gone but like Grandma used to say, 'You don't have to holler. God has big ears and can hear you if you whisper."

"All right, Ethel," I said, "let's get to the punchline. What's the greatest single influence in your life?"

"There has only been one," she answered, "Prayer."

"You mean anybody can do it?"

"Some folks are so heavenly-minded, they ain't any earthly good," she explained, "but if you pray and mean it, He can dry your eyes and wipe that sad look off your face. You don't have to join nothin'—and remember, the only dues to this union with God—is love."

"Gee, Ethel, you make it sound so easy."

"It is. It's easy to reach God—He's only a prayer away."

Chapter 12.

Let's Make a Deal

Any actor worth his weight in faith believes that God is love. God's work is done, it cannot be undone, it is forever complete. All we have to do is accept all the goodies he has laid out for us.

God does the healing and the helping and there is nothing too difficult for Him. He knows all, understands all, and is ever-present, ever ready to help with His inexhaustible supply of love.

Actors know this but they figure He could use a little help. So they carry rabbits' feet, four-leaf clovers, a cross and mezuzah, a St. Genesius (the patron saint of the arts), as well as a St. Christopher medal, even if it's out of fashion. They do benefits for Catholic, Protestant, Jewish and come-as-you-are causes just to keep in good. They live by their horoscopes and carry elephant hair bracelets or two teeth from an African tribe leader that was blessed by a witch doctor for luck, a bottle of holy water and an 8×10 enlargement of Golda Meir—autographed—anything to gain points with the Big Boss.

Even the unbelievers believe when they need a friend. The famed producer Max Gordon was never known for his

121

religious beliefs. Nobody ever saw him in church or a temple. One day, before the opening of one of his shows, he was running down the street when he bumped into Garson Kanin. "Where are you going in such a hurry?" the writer asked.

"I'm in a terrible hurry," he answered. "I'm on my way to the synagogue to do some praying."

"You? Pray?" Garson asked. "How come?"

"In case of a tie," Max answered, as he hurried away.

Perry Como always had his own personal priest with him whenever he performed. Father Bob, the-show business priest, and Como were an inseparable team. One day at Danny's Hideaway, Vic Damone walked in with a priest of his own and bumped into Mr. Nice Guy and Father Bob.

"Say," said Father Bob, "since when did you start palling around with a priest?"

"Since Perry made it," Vic answered. "If you can make him such a big star, you must have a pretty good connection. I figured I'd use somebody from the same agency."

Show people are always ready to make a deal with God and God, of course, is always ready to listen. One actor I know was in dire need of money. He hadn't worked in a year—not even as an Off-Broadway Santa Claus. He just couldn't leave the theater. "I'm married to it," he alibied.

"Then why don't you sue it for nonsupport," his wife suggested.

That's when he went to God. "Please—Lord—give me ten thousand dollars. I promise you on my career, if you'll just give me the money, I'll give half to charity."

He waited for a few seconds and when there was no response from above, he added, "Look, God, if you don't believe that I intend to give half to charity, then you divide it. Give me my five thousand now, and the other five thousand you can give to charity yourself. I trust you!"

You can bet your last bead that when God makes a deal he keeps it. That doesn't always happen with most of us, but in the case of actor Horace McMahon it was a contract that lasted a lifetime. Will Rogers once said, "I never met a man I

122

didn't like." Well, conversely, I never met a man, woman or child that didn't like Horace McMahon.

It was a full house at St. Joseph's church in Norwalk, Connecticut, which gave tribute to Horace when he took stage center for the last time at his requiem mass on August 20, 1971. In the audience were the big and the small of show business —all in harmony in their love for Horace. A love that had grown over the years in response to his friendship, kindness and humility in extending a helping heart wherever it was needed by whomever needed it.

I keep remembering Horace's advice to me always. "How can you love God whom you can't see if you don't love man whom you can see."

This love and affection for his fellow man and back to him came from a pact he made with the One who invented love and affection.

It all started for Horace on that memorable Christmas in 1931—or I should say it almost ended for him. It was Christmas Eve, and after trying agents and traveling to tryouts until he had walked himself two inches shorter and twenty pounds lighter, he faced the holidays broke and hungry. He was weary and empty as he looked out the window of his pitiful little room. It was snowing. He decided to go downstairs to the desk to pick up his mail.

The clerk gave him just one piece. It was a card expressing the warmest of Christmas greetings from the hotel. Stamped on the other side was a phrase not coined by the Wise Men— it said simply, "Please remit overdue bill."

Horace trudged back to his room, but his key would not open the door. He was locked out. Merry Christmas!

To top it off, he discovered he was in bigger trouble. No hard-hearted casting director or indifferent agent could knock him over. Tuberculosis did. And wouldn't you know it? While he was lying in the hospital, he got a call from an agent who offered him the part of his life in a new show opening on Broadway.

That's when our boy made his deal with the Biggest Agent

of them all. "If you get me out of here," he pleaded, "I promise You I'll be the greatest ad for You. I'll make you proud of me. I'll do your work for you on earth—and God, this is a run-of-the-play contract."

As always, God kept his part of the deal. Horace was better in days and went on to become the star of *Detective Story*, *Naked City*, and hundreds of other plays and pictures. Horace kept his part of the bargain, too. He brought a new meaning to the word friend. In loving respect to him I quote a favorite passage of his (Ecclesiastes 6:14–17):

"A faithful friend is a strong defense and he who hath found him found a treasure. Nothing can be compared to a faithful friend—and no weight of gold and silver is able to countervail the goodness of his fidelity. A faithful friend is the medicine of life and immortality. And they that fear the Lord shall find the faithful friend."

Another star who is always making deals with the Big Boss is Jacqueline Susann. The lady who sold more books than any female writer in the history of literature "joined the Agent in the Sky" when she was a little girl and heard the story in school from the Old Testament of how the people would sacrifice a basket from their best crops at an altar in thanks to God for the good harvest. And there was one man who thought, "Why burn good fruit?" So he filled the basket with overripe fruit and just covered the top with the good stuff. And when he put it on the altar, God smote the fruit and said: "That is no sacrifice —you are not giving up something that means a good deal to you."

"That story struck me when I was young," Jackie told me, "and I kept God very busy. If I passed in math, I would give up candy for a month. It always worked. Sometimes things piled up. Like I had sacrificed candy for a month and had two weeks to go and something else came up. Like I was swooning over some gawking fourteen-year-old on the high-school football team and longed for him to ask me to the school dance. So I'd offer up another sacrifice—and since I already had candy going for me—ice cream went next—then hot dogs—movies

124

only if it was someone like Frank Sinatra."

Jackie Susann has carried this thing all through her life. "I'm always making bargains with God," she told me. "I gave up drinking for Lent. One year I gave up hashed brown potatoes for twelve months. I promised God if I made the best-seller list with *Valley of the Dolls*, I'd give up smoking. Then I got so nervous going on talk shows I had a cigarette in both hands. So then I promised I'd give God a month for every week I stayed on the list. Well, who could have thought I'd be on it for sixty-five weeks? I was picking butts out of other people's ashtrays. It was disgusting."

The toughest trick for Our Lady of Smoking took place a few summers ago. I'll let her tell it to you herself. "I was in Paris and Irving and I decided to sail to New York on the *Liberté*. Percy Faith and a lot of our other friends were sailing on it and asked us to join them. Suddenly, with a passion more than anything in the world, we had to go by boat—and it would be the first time.

"This was a Monday and the boat was sailing Wednesday. We went to the French Line. They laughed at us. Reservations were impossible. Every boat on every line was sold out for months. Irving offered a bribe. Not a chance!

"I prayed. That night I sat in our living room of the George V after Irving went to bed and I promised God that if I got on the *Liberté*, the moment I learned of it, I would not smoke a cigarette for twenty-four hours. This for me was like saying I won't breathe for twenty-four hours. I'm the girl who smoked when I had pneumonia.

"Tuesday we called the French Line. No hope. And Tuesday night Percy Faith called us and told us that the sailing had been postponed for one day till Thursday. They had called him. So Wednesday morning we called, thinking maybe the delay might make someone want to fly back. Nothing! At noon we called again and Mr. Grevan, the Inspector-General said, 'Please forget it. It's a lovely day in Paris—go out and enjoy it. If anything comes up we will call you—but it's hopeless. The boat train leaves at eight tomorrow and it's noon now. No one has canceled. Forget it.'

125

"We went to the Louvre. I prayed before every religious painting I saw. When we came out I said to Irving, 'It's four. Let's go back to the hotel and see if there is any message.' He said, 'No, we're only a few blocks from the French Line—let's walk over.'

"I said, 'No,'—I'd be embarrassed—we've bothered them too much now—we have to have some dignity. Irving insisted that we walk over. Usually I can talk him out of anything, but this time he was adamant. So, we walked over. We got there at four-thirty. The Inspector-General was frantic. He had been calling the hotel for an hour. A first-class cancellation had turned up—and another couple was standing there waiting. He had been trying to contact us. They closed at five. If we hadn't walked in, the cabin would have gone to the other couple.

"I was smoking a cigarette. It was a quarter of five as Irving paid the money. I put out my cigarette and said to Irving, 'I promised God. I can't smoke now until tomorrow at a quarter to five.'

"Now Irving is not a big believer, yet a half hour later, as I unconsciously reached for a cigarette in the cab, he said, 'Hey, you can't smoke. You promised God.' I immediately put it back. I hadn't lit it.

"Now the torture started. Percy Faith threw a big party. It was a double celebration—our last night in Paris, and that we got on the boat. Oh, God. Sitting through cocktails and dinner without a cigarette. I thought I'd die. I also knew I'd never get through the twenty-four hours. But I was like an alcoholic or drug addict. I kept saying, 'It's ten o'clock now—only nineteen hours to go—I'll try and last till eleven without one.' At two A.M., when I got to sleep I was a wreck. I know what a dope fiend is like now.

"If only I had taken a sleeping pill and have slept till noon. But, no. At six I was up—to get ready for the boat train. And then coffee—Parisian coffee yet, which is palatable only with a cigarette. Yet I sat in bed without it.

"You are not an inveterate smoker, so you can't appreciate my feeling. But not to have a cigarette with the first cup of

126

coffee is like waking up and not brushing your teeth. And I sat and watched Irving smoke. I guess I looked so miserable that he said, 'O.K., you got through last night, which is enough. I release you from your oath.'

"I stared at him, then I said, '*You* release me? I didn't promise *you*—I promised *God*. How can *you* release me? Then the boat train. We sat in a compartment with another couple. Three hours—and everyone smoked.

"Percy Faith had one of those wrist watches with an alarm on it. Everyone knew about my oath. So, Percy set his alarm for a quarter to five. At four-thirty I took out a cigarette and carried it. I didn't light it. At a quarter of five I sat down and lit it, and felt I had accomplished the greatest feat of my life.

"And God paid me double-fold. It was the most fantastic trip I ever had. Anthony Quinn and all the stars danced attendance on me all the way. Maybe it wasn't right, but God works in his own way, and repays his flock with their own particular brand of enjoyment, as long as it doesn't hurt anyone else.

"He sure proved it to me many times. Only recently it was the big payoff. My husband had a polyp removed from his intestines. This time I went for the jackpot. I promised God if it wasn't malignant, I'd give up smoking for good. I finally made it."

Jackie says now that she bothers God only when it's absolutely necessary. "When I'm writing and it's not going well, I try the zoo. Seeing the animals helps. If that fails, then I bother God. Irving says I use the Lord like he was the William Morris Agency. But great as they are, they never accomplished the miracles of my 'Agent in the Sky.'"

I once asked Maurice Chevalier how it feels to be eighty-two and he said, "Considering the alternative . . . " When I asked Harry Hershfield what it was like to be eighty-eight, he answered, "I don't know—I was never eighty-eight before."

The incomparable Hildegarde is sixty-eight, going on thirty. She says it's because she talks to God. "That's what prayer is—contact with the Lord." And it's what keeps her so young.

When I asked Hildegarde what it was like to be sixty-eight and still going strong, she said, "It's serenity—which is what I talk to God about. And it happens to be the prayer I live by:

> Lord, give me the serenity to accept
>   the things I cannot change.
> The courage to change the things I can.
> And the wisdom to know the difference.

Hildegarde has been making deals with the Big Boss ever since she was a little girl in Milwaukee and realized He was listening. "If you get me an A in music, I promise I'll be an exemplary child," she promised. "I had some pretty good quarrels with Him, too," she told me, "when I didn't get what I deserved. But He's a good God and always made up with me."

When Hildy wanted to play her first concert in her home town, she worked overtime with God. "I really went all out this time," she told me. "I promised if He could book me for this one show, I would present my parish church with a life-sized statue of St. Theresa, the Little Flower, if it took me all my life to pay for it."

She must have gotten the job, because at St. Michael's in Milwaukee stands the most beautiful life-sized statue of St. Theresa. "It took me ten years to pay for it, but He kept his promise—and so did I," Hildegarde says. At sixty-eight she is still playing ball with the Lord. "I live my life," she says, "knowing there is another life ahead. This is a testing period."

Talking about deals, I must tell you the story of the rabbi at the Actor's Temple who spent most of the morning in fervent prayer. When he was finished, one of his richer but cheaper congregants remarked, "I hope you prayed for something specific—something that can do us some good."

"I did," the rabbi answered. "I prayed that the rich should give more to the poor."

"Let's hope God heard your prayers."

"I'm sure He did—at least half of it. The poor have agreed to accept the increase."

Then there's the story of the rich country singer who was kneeling in church trying to make a deal. "Please, God, I need another gold record—and while you're at it, can you throw in a picture deal? Also, I have only three houses now. Elvis has four. Would it be putting you out too much to get me another —with a pool?"

Kneeling next to him was a young chorus boy who was looking for his own deal. "Please, Sir, all I want is a job. Can you at least give me some break while I'm waiting—I'm hungry." The country singer, listening to all this, pulled a hundred-dollar bill out and said to the boy, "Here—don't bother Him with that small stuff."

When Harry Richman, one of the all-time superstars lost his money and his voice, he never blamed God. He just prayed every day, "If that's how you want it, Father, okay, but I'd rather sing than eat."

Any actor who would be hit with such a parlay ain't gonna be too happy—but to Richman it was a catastrophe. Harry drank too much, gambled too much and played too much—but as he said proudly, "It was a hell of a life."

Harry Richman was a pilot, an amateur boxer, a fisherman of record, a star, a lover of note and the greatest partygiver of all time. His friends were the millionaires of the town as well as the gangsters, athletes, authors, the most beautiful women in the world, Presidents, ambassadors, royalty and Bowery bums—and Richman was always the host.

When he was completely broke and didn't know where and if the next booking was coming or the next meal, a group of his buddies decided to run a benefit for him. I came to him with the news while he was in the hospital. "Sinatra, Tony Martin, Hy Gardner and I are working on a TV and record deal in your honor. We are going to get the greatest singing stars in America and Europe to sing the songs you introduced and all the profits will go to you—it could be as much as a quarter of a million dollars. Tell me, how will you invest the money— what will you do with it?"

"I'll blow it all on the biggest party the world has ever seen," he answered.

"Harry Richman wears Broadway like a boutonniere," Eddie Cantor said of him. Walter Winchell said, "Harry lights up the sky wherever he goes."

Harry was always a sucker for a sad story or a beautiful girl. Almost every night he would walk into the most expensive joints in town, with a girl to match on each arm, and blow the whole bankroll. Nobody tipped bigger than our hero.

I was with him one time at the Copacabana when he approached the headwaiter and asked, "What's the biggest tip you ever got?"

"One hundred dollars," the man at the door said.

"Okay," Harry said, "here's two hundred bucks—meet the new champ."

"Thank you so much, Mr. Richman," the man said. "I'll never forget you."

"By the way," Harry asked, "who is it that gave you the hundred?"

"You did," the headwaiter answered.

Harry really led a hell of a life—but now it was over and he did the only thing he could do—he went to God. "Look," he said, "I'm not complaining. All I want is my voice back and I promise I'll be your greatest salesman. I'll use it to only praise You."

Naturally, God put him back together again as he does to anybody that comes looking for Him. When his voice returned, Harry told me, "I realized I'd been to many doctors but none worked as perfectly as the Great Healer."

For his new engagement, Richman had star billing deleted from his contract. "There's only one Headliner," he explained. "The rest of us are only added attractions."

Chapter 13.

———◦⚬∞⚬◦———

In Thy Pure Sight

Let my ways be justified
  In Thy pure sight alone;
Not in the sight of men, O Lord,
  Nor even in my own.

The eyes of others may mistake,
  Their judgment err and fail;
And sin or will may dim my own,
  For human sense is frail.

But thoughts that dwell in holiness,
  And words that speak Thy might,
Will justify themselves, and so
  Find blessing in Thy sight!

Kathryn Paulson Grounds

That poem really tells it like it is. All you have to do is please that Audience of One. Let's face it—if God is with you, who can be against you?

He is the Producer as well as the Critic. And your best Audience. After all, He made you in the first place. You are His child—and He's very proud of you. He's not going to let you bomb out if you come to Him for advice and help.

And remember that God made you an individual. He never made any carbons—and like it says in the Good Book, He looked at everything that He had made and it was very good.

So don't try to copy anybody else. Do it your way—because it's His way. Don't envy anybody else. Envy is the game of counting the other guy's blessings instead of your own. You are loaded with individual blessings. Count them out loud. It's the best way you can look good in His pure sight.

Whether going on stage or in the factory, do your highest sense of right, which is His highest sense of right—and you can't miss. "You gotta believe," and you've got it licked. Remember, you are possessed of His goodness, living in His harmonious realm, governed by His law.

"The Lord is my light and my salvation; whom shall I fear? The Lord is the strength of my life; of whom shall I be afraid?" (Psalms 27:1)

Singing star Anita Bryant told one critic, "I'm really only accountable to my father—I mean, my Heavenly Father."

The critic wanted to know if she wasn't a fanatic about her religion.

"Well," Anita explained, "fanatic is just like a fan, isn't it? It's the same root, I think. I am the Lord's greatest fan—so I guess I am a fanatic."

The Big Boss is always near to those who believe in Him and depend on Him.

Dale Evans Rogers told me a story that proves this truth. "My husband and I were working on a record when a secretary handed me a message. It said: "Mrs. Roy Rogers, call Italy, Texas. Urgent! The telephone number given me was that of my brother. My heart sank as I thought of my eighty-three-year-old mother, who was in a rest home there.

"Breathing a quick prayer for courage, I dialed the number. My sister-in-law answered, and in a strange, quiet voice

134

told me my brother, my only one, had just passed away from a heart attack in a hotel room in New York. He was fifty-six years old.

"One night soon after his funeral, I was unable to sleep. In tears, I started to pray, beseeching the Lord for some sign of comfort for my aching heart. I lay there under the covers, waiting, looking to the Lord expectantly for what He had promised—'I will come to you.' (John 14:18)

"Suddenly, I felt a firm but gentle pressure on my entire body, as if invisible hands had soothed me in assurance that all was well. I knew with sudden clarity that the spirit of my beloved brother had returned to God. And I slept."

This is the prayer that Dale Evans Rogers passes on to you: "I thank Thee, Oh Lord, for Thy comforting presence in every time of need, and for the assurance that Thou doest all things well. Amen."

Madame Chiang Kai-Shek told me, "We Chinese have a saying: 'If a man plants melons, he will reap melons; if he sows beans, he will reap beans.' And this is true of every man's life; good begets good, and evil leads to evil.

"It is true that the sun shines on saint and sinner alike, and sometimes it seems that the wicked prosper, but you can be sure that, with the individual, as well as with the nation, the flourishing of the wicked is an illusion, for, unceasingly, life keeps books on us all."

My friend Madame Chiang Kai-Shek will be happy to know that, even before her time, the Bible said it pretty well: ". . . whatsoever a man soweth, that shall he also reap." (Galatians 6:7)

Barbara Walters, the NBC star reporter of 'The Today Show' never had any religious training—even in her family life. But when she grew up she began questioning the whys and wherefores of things and the realities of existence. "I suddenly realized I had no formation of God in my mind. To me He was a mortal, with a long white beard who lived on a cloud."

But when she became a reporter and she started searching, she found that she could talk to God. "Now I believe in Him. I haven't called on Him in terms of career or unfolding or development in my life, but I have never gone into an airplane without thanking Him first. I always have a dialogue with him, or really, a monologue. I thank Him in advance for my blessings for the safe trip I know He is going to see that I have.

"Another area in which I always seem to be in communication with Him is with my five-year-old daughter, Jacqueline. I thank Him for her health, for her perfection.

"Of course, I believe. I'm a thorough reporter and I know a good thing when I see it—when I feel it—when I call on Him.

"I don't beseech Him or beg Him or implore or petition Him to make things better and I haven't always had things going well. Like everyone else I've had difficult periods in my life. However, when I reach out and up in times of great happiness, it's thanking Him for everything He's given me so far—and will in the future."

The beloved singer, Marion Anderson, recalled to me a blessed gift from her mother. "The faith that my mother taught me is my foundation. It is the only ground on which I stand. With it I have a freedom in my life I could not have in any other way. Whatever is in my voice, my faith has put it there."

Marion attended a Baptist church in Philadelphia as a little girl, sang in the church choir and even did a solo once in a while. But her mother taught her that the form of one's faith is less important than what's in one's heart.

"When you come to Him," Mom told her, "He never asks what you are."

Marion told me that a lot of people helped her in her career. When she flopped at one Town Hall concert, she was ready to give it all up. "I felt I let Mom and all my friends

136

down," she told me. "I told my mother I'd better forget about singing and do something else."

"Why don't you think about it a little," Mom cautioned, "and pray about it a lot, before you make any decision."

Marion realized then, from her torment, that even the most self-sufficient cannot find enough strength to stand alone. Then, one prays with a fervor one never had before. "I prayed," Marion told me, "with the sure knowledge there was Someone to Whom I could pour out the greatest need of my heart and soul. It did not matter if He answered. It was enough to pray.

"I came out of my despair—my mind began to clear— self-pity left me. I ran to my mother and shouted joyously, 'I want to study again. I want to be the best, I want to be loved by everyone, and be perfect in everything.' "

Mom said lovingly, "That's a beautiful goal, but our dear Lord walked the earth as the most perfect of all beings, yet not everybody loved Him."

"My prayers have been answered," Marion told her mother, "I know now I can't fail."

"Mine, too," Mom said. "Prayer begins where human capacity ends."

I saw Marion Anderson recently at former Governor Rockefeller's dinner table and we talked about her great success. "I am so grateful," she told me, "for my career and all the goodies that come with it. If sometimes I do not hear the echo and listen only to the applause, my mother reminds me quickly of what should come first. 'Grace must always come before greatness.' "

It doesn't matter what tongue you use, or what your needs are. God keeps you in focus in His pure sight—if you come to Him with grace and love.

There is an old Scottish prayer that says: "God help the poor—for the rich can help themselves."

And an old English prayer which says: "God help the rich —for the poor can beg."

My favorite morning prayer is from Psalms 117: "This is

137

the day which the Lord hath made: let us be glad and rejoice therein."

George Herbert comes up with a thankful prayer: "O God, thou hast given so much to us, give one thing more—a grateful heart. Amen."

The Chinese have a special prayer: "I shall be true—for there are those that trust me."

St. Francis of Assisi had us all in mind with this prayer:

"Lord, make me an instrument of Thy Peace. Where there is hatred, let me sow love. Where there is injury, pardon. Where there is doubt, faith. Where there is despair, hope. Where there is darkness, light. Where there is sadness, joy.

"O Divine Master, grant that I may not so much seek to be consoled as to console; to be understood as to understand; to be loved, as to love; for it is in giving that we receive, it is in pardoning that we are pardoned, and it is in dying that we are born to eternal life."

Lawrence Welk says that faith in God gives us faith in ourselves and others. Here is his favorite prayer: "Lord, without reservation I trust in Your Power. Help me to back up my faith with positive action. In faith I open the door. Show me the way. Amen."

Circle one, check a box, pick the prayer you like. Or make one up of your own—as long as you humble yourself before Him. Harry Hershfield tells us about a very devout man who found himself and his family uprooted and without a morsel of food. His wife pleaded "Please, you are a Holy Man. Ask God to help us." Her husband answered, "Foolish woman—I must do God's will, but I have no right to ask God to do my will."

If you have faith and a sense of humor—and they go together—you can't hurt yourself, even if you try. God is watching over you, talking to you, showing you the way. All you have to do is tune Him in.

I keep laughing at the story of the disgruntled old man who wanted to give up. He stretched himself across the railroad tracks with a loaf of bread under his arm. A policeman happened to pass by, and asked, "What do you think you're doing?"

"Waiting for the train to run over me—I do not wish to live any longer," the man said.

"But why the loaf of bread?" the puzzled policeman asked.

"The way the trains run here," the man answered tartly, "you could starve to death waiting for one."

Not everybody is a headliner—but *everybody* is a star with the Head Man. You don't need top billing to impress Him, all you need is the desire and the love. As one Hasidic student put it, "Would I could love the best of men as tenderly as God loves the worst."

Which is a segue into the story of the hard-working man who came to his rabbi for help. "I don't get it," he pleaded. "I have labored hard and long in the service of the Lord, and yet I have received no improvement. I am still an ordinary and ignorant person."

The rabbi answered, "You have gained the realization that you are ordinary and ignorant, and this in itself is a worthy accomplishment."

Composer Burt Bacharach told me, "I can think of no occupation that compares to the music business where the participants can be so high on a cloud of accomplishment one day, and so low in frustration the next. As far as the writing of music is concerned, it is an accepted fact that the success or failure of a song is almost completely unpredictable."

I guess that's where you separate the big-time from the small-time. The recipe is faith.

"Some of the songs I've written," Burt told me, "seemed to promise that they would be big hits—and they actually turned out to be big bombs. Others just didn't seem to have enough potential, and were kept in the proverbial 'bottom of the trunk,' before being offered to a publisher.

"The best example of the latter, which Hal David and I

139

didn't think had a chance, was 'What the World Needs Now is Love.' "

Much earlier in Burt's career, there were long, dry spells when he was often tempted to give up his music bit. He thought about being a sportscaster, a jockey, a clothing salesman, and a hundred other things, but he was "hooked" on music, and nothing could shake his faith that he could develop into a successful composer.

Of course, he had a couple of people who had a lot of faith in him, too. His mother and father. "In those early days," Burt says, "I had and still have, a pair of parents who backed me up with music lessons, attendance at summer music camps, a special course with Darius Milhaud, plus a grand piano when the family could least afford that luxury. But they had their faith that I could succeed. And later my dear wife Angie and now my daughter Nikki had their faith. Come to think of it, I've been heartened by that faith—a kind of faith based on hard work and the blessings I've received."

Burt Bacharach, Burt's father, and a columnist, author and commentator in his own "write," tells me that he always had faith in his Burt. "I always felt Somebody up there was looking out for him.

"I'm not superstitious, but if you observe me closely in times of stress, you might notice that I occasionally knock on wood. The only explanation I can give of that is, it is probably an unconscious effort to get the attention of Somebody Up There who will help me. And He always does."

Danny Thomas says: "Me? I'm a philosophizing bum—but I promised God, 'Help me find my place in life, and I will build you a shrine where the poor, the helpless and the hopeless may come for comfort and aid.'

"My purpose in life is to propagate the philosophy of Man's faith in Man, based upon my own belief that unless Man reestablishes faith in his fellow beings, he can never establish a faith in God.

"In order that others who follow may be inspired to do

140

likewise I have to leave something. I'm not so unforgettable that I could do it only with words. I must leave something that men can touch, feel, see. That will be the St. Jude Research Hospital in Memphis, Tennessee."

The beloved Eleanor Roosevelt once told me, "The way your personal religion makes you live is the only thing that matters. Life is meant to be lived as fully and as happily as possible. In addition to prayer and congregational worship, I have found the Holy Bible a remarkably wise and beautiful book—and reading a few verses every day a helpful habit."

When I asked her what her favorite verses were, she answered readily, "In First Corinthians Chapter Thirteen it starts, 'Though I speak with the tongues of men and of angels, and have not charity, I am become as sounding brass or a tinkling cymbal.' And then it ends so beautifully, 'Now abideth faith, hope and charity, these three; but the greatest of these is charity!'"

Eddie Cantor lived by these words. It was Cantor who started the March of Dimes in honor of Franklin Delano Roosevelt, and like the beautiful Eleanor Roosevelt, he never stopped running. He was always in a hurry to reach the top.

I visited him in his Beverly Hills home when he was near the end. He was tired and ill, but certainly not ready to give up. "What piece of advice could you give a young fellow starting out now?" I asked him.

"The same advice my grandmother gave me a long time ago, which I wish I had followed. 'Don't go too fast, son,' she used to say, 'or you'll miss the scenery.' I paid no attention. When a man knows where he's going, why waste time getting there?

"I'd give anything to back up a little now, and take time out to enjoy my family and friends and some of the little things along the way—that you don't get to do when you're running too fast—seeing nothing but the finish line.

"My advice to you—don't do what I did. Don't go too fast —or you'll miss all that beautiful scenery."

The only consolation we have when we lose a loved one, is the good we did for them while they were with us. Beautiful and talented June Lockhart must have remembered that when she was called to the bedside of her father Gene Lockhart.

June and Gene were a great father-daughter team on stage and off.

She said later, "As I sat there watching my dear father slip away, a strange sense of peace came over me." A short time after that, June was able to put this feeling of peace into words. Although very personal to her, I'm sure she would want me to tell it here, in the hope that it may be helpful to others faced with the loss of a loved one:

> I cannot grieve
> My spirit is too full
> I've known my soul's elation
> Since his death
>
> Heart's joy
> There were no omissions . . .
> Our lives filled with each other . . .
> No word unsaid—no thought unfinished
> No love unknown
>
> I cherish his sharp moments
> His anxiety for faith
> Our mutual impatience—disagreements
> All these are father-daughter fabric.
>
> He gave his father-love
> And carried me to independent womanhood.
> Such an entity am I
> At his death my being stands strong
> Alone
>
> There is no wound—no tie to sever
> It is a blessed loss
> And I am peaceful

And what did I give him?
All that I should—
I dearly loved him

I cannot grieve
My spirit is too full.
I've known my soul's elation
Since his death.

When columnist, lecturer and crusading reporter Victor Riesel was blinded by a gangster who hurled acid in his face, he could have resorted to self-pity, bitterness and hate. "But in the darkness," Victor told me, "it slowly came to me that what happens to a man isn't nearly as important as how he meets it."

Victor found a world of love in the midst of his tragedy. Hundreds of people offered their eyes, including one mother of three who said she gladly offered him one of her eyes because she could not rear her children without some protest against such enormous evil. "This torrent of generosity," Victor told me, "was in itself a humbling experience."

The President of the United States, the press, people everywhere offered their help. "And through it all," Victor says, "I, the son of a Jewish needleworker, felt the merciful hands of the nuns who run St. Clare's Hospital.

"Some of us can be articulate about our personal faith. I cannot. The best I can say is that deep within us are the resources to face any calamity without being crushed by it. If we look hard enough, each of us can find a faith to feed our deepest needs."

"When you realized that you could never see again," I asked Victor, "were you bitter? Did you feel that you were abandoned?"

"On the contrary," he answered. "As I lay there in great pain, I felt a hand on my shoulder. I felt God had saved me for something more important—to fight for little people against the power-crunching guys.

"You see," he explained, "you either think of your life as

143

half-empty or half-filled. Mine is half-filled with spirit and faith in the will to do my Father's bidding."

"You see better than all of us," I said.

"Well," he explained, "blind, I am less dazzled by material things. I have a deeper hunger for blazing light which the right always needs. Even in the darkness, I can see the light."

"Did you always believe?" I asked.

"Being a hard-nosed realistic cynical reporter, I investigated the God bit like I would a union contract—and I realized for the first time that I could see better without eyes. I looked for the beginning, how it all started. No human could have done it. It must be the Almighty. Where is the beginning? Where is the endless end? That's when I saw God. I don't know His shape or features, but I do know that without Him there is no beginning, no end, and no in-between.

"I also know that when I walked out of that hospital, His hand was guiding me, and has been with me ever since."

Beautiful and talented singing star Helen O'Connell had an eye operation recently. For eight days she lay there with her eyes bandaged, without a drop of light coming in or out. "I knew when they peeled off those covers," she told me later, "I would see perfectly. I had talked to God in advance and thanked Him, He told me it would be okay—and you can bet he wouldn't let me down."

Mary Martin has always lived with the prescription, "Every wish is like a prayer to God." The story of Peter Pan says, "Wishes are thoughts vibrant with life and eager for action. They have the power to produce light and beauty."

It's only wonderful to extend good wishes to your friends and relations on holidays and especially at the New Year. "But," says Mary Martin, "it's even more important to extend best wishes to ourselves—wish them to yourself with all your heart—and strive toward them with all your might."

And I've got some real hot news for you—the prayer bit

144

works. Just make sure those wishes are important to you. He has a way of making them come true.

I have a special bulletin for you. Don't wish too hard unless you really mean it. There is an old Talmudic story of a poor man who had to carry an unbearable load on his back. One day when he could carry it no farther, he cried out in despair, "Oh, Death—come and free me."

In a flash the Angel of Death was at his side asking politely, "You called for me?"

"Yes," the poor man answered hastily, "please help me put my load back on my shoulders."

Chapter 14.

Alan Young

Alan Young gave up show business to work full-time as a Christian Science practitioner. Even in the early days, when he was the star of the "Mr. Ed" show, he might have been talking to the horse but he was listening for God.

"I remember while filming one of the 'Ed' series," Alan was telling me one day, "I overheard the cast and crew talking about someone backstage, 'He's a real nut—this guy's a Christian Scientist, you know,' and they went on to knock this particular character, stressing the fact that he was such a kook. I mustered up all my nerve and said, 'Hey, fellas, I don't want to bother you, but so am I. I'm one of those kooks. I'm a Christian Scientist.'"

There's something about being a Christian Scientist—in show business—that attracts all the hecklers. Because Christian Scientists don't believe in doctors or sickness, it brings out everybody's worst jokes. "If the cost of medicine and doctors keeps going up," one chorus girl cried, "we'll all have to become Christian Scientists."

One actor reported that he knows a vandal who got tired

of painting swastikas on synagogues, so now he's painting R_x signs on Christian Science Reading rooms.

Alan tells me that the line thrown at him the most is: "Hey, you're a Christian Scientist? Do you mind changing places with me? I'm sitting in a draft."

Alan very often lives with us when he's in New York, and I can tell you firsthand that he works at being a good Scientist. He says his prayers the first thing every morning and does his lessons by reading the Bible and *Science and Health with Key to the Scriptures,* by Mary Baker Eddy. Lately I noticed that he was reading the newspapers first before he did his lessons.

"Are prayers less important?" I heckled him.

"Not at all," he explained. "I'm just looking to see what I have to pray about—and believe me, with all the scandals going on these days I know God is saying, 'Now are you ready to listen to me?'"

If Christian Science brings out the worst in comics, it brings out the best in Scientists. Mary Baker Eddy once said, "There are wit, humor and enduring vivacity among God's people—and a dose of joy is a spiritual cure."

Alan, like most Scientists, enjoys the barbs as well as the gags. Says our hero, "I think every morning people should pray for a sense of humor tempered with kindness because it negates bitterness, anger and everything opposite to joy. Joy, like health, is a spiritual quality. It doesn't need any human or physical circumstance to bring it about. It's here. We have a sense of humor just as we have a sense of health. I think true joy results in good humor. And how many times a laugh has healed! I've been suddenly healed by laughing at mortal mind because it was so ridiculous."

"There was a period I drifted away from Christian Science," Alan recalls. "It was ten years long. But even while drifting away I was only giving myself excuses because in the back of my mind I knew this life couldn't be for me. I blamed everything I was doing on the fact that there was so much gung-ho, go-go-go fun in Hollywood all around me and I'd never sampled it. And then I felt that this religion of mine was sort of keeping me from trying all this great stuff that the world had to offer. I figured it was hypocritical to stay in church and act like I was acting, so I drifted away. I drank, smoked, went the whole route. But always in the back of my mind I figured I could stop any time. But I soon discovered I couldn't. I was by then drinking so much that I had a serious alcoholic problem. And I, by then, thoroughly enjoyed boozing so much that I needed pills to put me to sleep and then pills to wake me up. My doctor bills were breaking me. And the more I went to the doctors, the less they could do for me. I was sick, and the doctor kept telling me there was nothing wrong that he could find. My wife had been studying Christian Science at that point and she said one day, "Listen, boy, it's either an MD or a practitioner. Take your choice." So she sent for a practitioner. He was a young boy. Lean, good-looking. It could have been me walking in. He prayed for me and the next time I reached for a cigarette it tasted terrible. The drink tasted terrible."

Once Alan decided to quit show business and become a practitioner, the offers really started to come in. Two months after he left Hollywood he was given the best offer he ever had. He was really tempted until the next day. "I had a case," says our star, "where somebody needed help badly. I healed him and I realized then that this was the biggest thrill of all. It was bigger than any round of applause I ever received."

The Alan Young story is beautiful. I think I ought to let him tell it himself:

"My dad decided to leave the comparative ease of English living and move family and belongings to the New World. We hit Western Canada first, and Western Canada hit back. Always a little ahead of the pack, Dad succeeded in losing his shirt five years before the Crash. He was out of work, broke, with a sick wife and two children. My mother was beginning to get the idea that 'somebody up there doesn't like us,' when a lady dropped by with different news. She told us of a God who wasn't 'up there' somewhere but was an ever-available loving Guide and Healer. She told my mother a little about Christian Science, gave her some literature and left.

"At times like this the stories tell of a bright light descending, angel voices singing, instantaneous healings, and human wealth beyond measure. It didn't happen like that in our case. We got something much greater. We saw *hope*. We saw that God was not a finite being bestowing gifts according to pleading or a formal father raging, punishing, condemning, and eventually forgiving and lifting into some other world at some other time. We saw a Father-Mother God who loved us *now*. Our lot began to improve. My mother's health was restored, Dad's work increased. None of this happened magically but gradually and magnificently.

"Sometime later, I was struck with what appeared to be chronic asthma. After a particularly unpleasant bout with this difficulty and a couple of added complications, my mother decided to send me to a Christian Science nursing home where I would be cared for properly. I arrived at the home an emaciated, frail-looking object. As someone later described it, 'You looked like something the cat dragged in, locked out, and then dragged out again.' The head nurse was a happy type, loving, sympathetic, but unimpressed by this woeful picture standing in front of her. She was also very busy as the sanitorium was understaffed, small, and had great demands on it. She also knew that I needed encouragement and needed it fast.

" 'Well, dear,' she said, 'I hope you claim your healing quickly because we need the sheets.' Her absolute faith that I could be healed whenever I decided to claim it woke me up. Her humor gave me a much-needed lift. Suddenly, I wasn't afraid any more. That night when the physical difficulty became activated, I began to read *Science and Health with Key to the Scriptures*, by Mary Baker Eddy, and began earnestly to put into practice the method of thinking this book teaches. In the morning I was well. Almost immediately I began to do chores around the sanitorium, not so much to attempt to pay for my keep as to simply express my gratitude. Within a week I was riding a bicycle and working as strongly as the healthiest member of the staff.

"Six weeks later I stumbled onto my career. It was a different seventeen-year-old returning home from the nursing sanitorium. It was early evening and I was spending the five-hour boat ride sitting on the top deck, looking out over the

152

dark ocean. A friendly little lady spoke to me for awhile and asked me what I was going to do with my life. I really hadn't given it much thought; I was grateful to be alive. After she left, the question puzzled me. What was I going to do with my life and career? I realized that God wouldn't heal me to leave me groping around picking up the pieces for the rest of my life. God is Love and doesn't take us half way. I looked up at the wheelhouse of the boat. It was completely dark. I realized that inside was the captain with a chart and a compass. Those were his guides. Even though it was black outside and he couldn't see the way, he knew that if he stuck with these immediate guides—his chart and compass—he'd find his port. This, then, was my answer. I would do the nearest thing to what was right, stick to my chart, which was trust in God, and I, too, would find my port.

"When I arrived home, I decided I would express love wherever possible. I found that one of my neighbors had a sick child and had been nursing him day and night. I went to her and said I would be happy to sit with him and read to him while she went out and did her shopping or got her hair done or simply went for a walk. It was while reading to this young boy that the telephone rang. The program director of a local radio station was calling. He had heard me give a comic recitation the year before, remembered it, and asked if I would care to do it that coming Saturday on a new program he was starting up. I did the show and was asked back for the following week. After the show had run a year and I knew the program director fairly well, I asked him how he had located me that night. 'I just got your number and called you,' he said. 'But I wasn't at home,' I said. He thought for a minute and then replied, 'Well, I really don't know how I got your number. Is it important?' I agreed that it wasn't important. We spend so much time figuring how God can possibly do something that we don't recognize the fact that He has already done it.

About this time, I hit the manager of the station for a raise. I told him I felt the three dollars he was paying me for writing and performing in the show was not enough and I should get five. His answer was short and quick. 'For five dollars I can hire a cowboy singer. They yodel and play the guitar.'

"Surprisingly, being fired didn't discourage me. I had a feeling that this was all a part of the divine plan. I had a purpose along with my identity and nobody could take my purpose from me nor separate it from my identity. We shouldn't cling to jobs simply because they feel comfortable or make us feel happy. We don't feel sad when the blossoms fall off the trees. They have to go because the fruit is coming. I felt that the loss of this job was simply the blossom falling off and that I had something great in store for me. I realized I must diversify. I learned to yodel and play the bagpipes, then put together an act and got a job with a small vaudeville group.

"Opening night for me was a disaster. It wasn't a debut, it was a debris! Three seats got up and walked out. An experienced old Scottish clog dancer got me backstage after the show. 'Son,' he said, 'it doesn't make any difference if your act is good or bad. First, you've got to make them love you.' So that night when I came on stage, I was smiling. I didn't start my act until I stood there and smiled. I smiled at the cheap seats, I smiled at the orchestra, I smiled at the walls. I'd show them I loved them! They thought I was an idiot. Again I bombed.

"The next show, I figured I'd make it plainer. I'd tell them that I loved them. 'Ah, I love ya,' was my opening line. 'I love your town, I love your weather, I love your streets.' This was a bleak, cold, mining town in northern British Columbia. Even its founding fathers couldn't stand it. Now the audience knew I was being a phony. That night I did what I should have done at the beginning. I prayed. I asked God to teach me to love—not to love persons, people, audiences, just to love. The flower doesn't wait until somebody gets close to it before giving off its perfume. It gives it off continually because that's its identity. I must love because Love was my identity. I realized the audiences weren't there to hate me. They were coming to see happiness expressed and I realized that through expressing God I could express love and happiness. And, of course, it began with loving my audience. If I love them, I can make them happy. That night, the act went over very well.

"The term 'lucky break' is used to explain the successful

154

accomplishments of many performers. Looking at my own theatrical history, I see so many of these remarkable developments that only the most fatalistic agnostic could refer to them as 'lucky breaks.' It seemed that the top of the heap in the entertainment world was the United States, and in my case it was reaching the point where this step was imminent. But how to make the jump to a country that had never heard of you?

"In New York an agent, Frank Cooper, was listening to a radio program called 'Chamber Music of Lower Basin Street.' A writer he handled was writing the show and as a faithful agent, he was checking his client's work. Suddenly there was a peculiar static noise in his radio. He heard laughter but the people speaking had what he called funny dialects. He held on to the dial of his radio until the end of the show and got the name of the performer and learned it was Toronto, Canada, and the performer's name was Alan Young. He wrote a letter to me inviting me to come down to the United States to replace Eddie Cantor for the summer. I did so. Visiting Frank's home one day, he pointed to a little portable radio he had shoved up on the shelf of his closet. 'That's the one I picked you up on,' he said. 'I was tuned in to a local New York station and it jumped to Toronto, Canada, over five hundred miles away. Incidentally,' he said, 'it's never worked since. I can't get the part for it and I'm keeping it as sort of a memento of our association.'

"To me the entertainment world is the greatest. I jump to my feet when 'There's No Business Like Show Business' blares forth! It's a stirring anthem. I suppose it would be my sole allegiance if I hadn't heard 'Onward, Christian Soldiers,' first. While I loved everything I did in show business, there was always the deep feeling that the ultimate was not universal stardom, a roomful of Emmys, Oscars and Pulitzer Prizes, and a standing pass to the Ice Follies. My desire was that sometime I might gratefully serve the Christian Science movement. Just over two years ago, we rented a house on the eastern seaboard far from Hollywood and New York, and I took time out to sit on the rock overlooking the ocean, doing light thinking, heavy praying, and I trust, obedient listening. The time had come, as

155

Paul said, 'forgetting those things which are behind, and reaching forth unto those things which are before, [to] press toward the mark for the prize of the high calling of God in Christ Jesus.'

"All the applause is great as a means of telling you that your work has been accepted, but there is no greater thrill, satisfaction, and gratitude than knowing that you are in the right place, doing your right thing. It was well said by somebody that we must listen and obey, but we must also go further than that and be quick to obey, for if we listen and are quick to obey, then our life can be a revelation instead of a revolution."

Chapter 15.

Archie Bunk, or Debunking Archie

Archie Bunk is alive and not well and won't live too long if we laugh him out of space.

Archie Bunker and his crowd are laughing all the way to the bank—at the haters and troublemakers—because they know that faith will overcome them all.

Now, what has faith to do with laughter?

Ask anyone who has felt the oppressor's lash, and it makes no difference whether he is Protestant, Catholic or Jew, he must answer: "Laughter is a weapon which leaves the oppressor helpless, and it is a shield of the spirit which defeats him."

All the haters and bullies are like the lion of the ancient fable. The lion swaggered through the jungle, showing off his strength, and roared at the tiger, "Who is the king of the jungle?"

"You are, of course, oh mighty lion," the tiger answered. The lion approached in turn the zebra, the buffalo and the leopard with the same question. All three readily agreed that the lion was, indeed, king of all the beasts. But when the lion roared at the elephant, "Who is king of the jungle?" he was picked up quickly by the elephant's trunk, battered against a tree and dropped, contemptuously, to the ground.

Whereupon the lion whined, "Just because you don't know the answer, you don't have to lose your temper."

At their doom, all of history's tyrants, bigots and bullies learn too late that the bodies of free men may be overcome, but their spirit is unconquerable.

Yet, unwittingly, the evil that tyrants have done has sometimes created a good that lives after them. From oppression came the endless streams of humanity that made America.

My beautiful friend Harry Hershfield says, "What is America if not a flight for freedom? What is the strength of its people if not a providential blend of nationalities? When they came they all marched with God, and a people whose spirit marches with God always has the gift of laughing at adversity."

"Then was our mouth filled with laughter, and our tongue with singing: Then said they among the Heathen, The Lord hath done great things for them." (Psalms 126:2)

There is an old Hasidic saying which goes like this: "To love God truly, one must first love man. And if anyone tells you that he loves God and does not love his fellow men, you will know that he is lying."

This all leads to the Greatest Story Ever Told, of how one reporter debunked an entire community by laughing at them right out loud in hundreds of newspapers around the world. The headline said: 2000 YEARS LATER AND STILL NO ROOM AT THE INN——ON THE LINE—*By Bob Considine.*

He had grown a bit older through the nearly 2,000 years. He had been working too hard. The phones had been going night and day for centuries. There were millions of newcomers He had not been able to meet as yet.

His Mother was the first to notice the gray around His temples. Quietly, firmly, she suggested that He get away for a spell, and just before His birthday as a Man the suggestion was accepted.

He went to the window of His study one clear night and looked things over, seeking a vacation spot. There were billions of places to tempt Him, but after a bit, a distant

160

memory stirred itself, and searching the littered sky, He found a tiny, luminous cinder amid an obscure constellation out on the end of creation. And He remembered its name: Earth.

His Mother was a bit vexed by His choice of a place to spend the holiday.

"The hotel situation is bad there," she reminded Him. "Don't you remember all that trouble we had getting reservations?"

He laughed a little in His kindly way and assured her that nearly 2,000 years can make a lot of changes in man's hostility to man. She went off to pack for Him, and pretty soon Michael, the swiftest of his archangels, walked in.

"I heard You're going on a trip," the archangel said. "I'll fly You down. In that way I'll be handy in case You need me."

"No thanks, Michael," He said. "I'll get down, all right. Besides, I've been wanting to try some of the transportation down there. Primitive, isn't it?"

And it came to pass that on the morning before Christmas, He arrived in New York City, bought some clothes that conformed to what the natives were wearing, and hopped a jet for Gold Beach, Fla. The travel poster had looked so nice.

An odd thing happened at the first hotel. "All booked," the clerk said, after a snobbish glance. It was that same way at the next four places, but the doorman at the last place took an interest in Him. "Your best bet is a motel, Mac," the man said. "They're not so hoity-toity."

He did, indeed, find a room at a motel; a room and astonishingly, an invitation to cocktails and dinner. The manageress "moonlighted" in supplying rich Gold Beach dowagers with extra men, there being a man shortage.

It was a grand party in a spacious old home and He found it stimulating. Nobody caught His name, but He passed that off as one of the idiosyncrasies of this odd little planet. The talk was fine: Certain political events had stirred the men; fashion events, the women.

Everything would have gone nicely, he supposed later, if the talk had not turned to, "Where are You from?" They were from an interesting variety of places that had sprung

161

up during the split seconds of the last two or three centuries. Then, just before the party was to move on to the exclusive Wampum Club for dinner, somebody asked Him where He was from.

"I was born in Bethlehem," He said. "It's a small place."

"Bethlehem," his host repeated. "Spent a lot of time there when I was in steel. Fine town!"

"Then we moved to a town named Nazareth and finally to Jerusalem," He said.

To His wonder, that portion of the room fell silent. The host was the first to recover. He boomed for another round of drinks, took the Stranger by the arm and escorted Him to a sitting room.

"That's very interesting . . . Bethlehem, Nazareth, Jerusalem," he said, lighting a cigar. "What's your profession?"

"I was a carpenter in those days," He said, with a smile. "Then I sort of went on the road, as you say."

"Salesman?"

"Yes, I guess you could call it that."

"We thought You were some kind of a writer, from the beard."

He shook His head. "No, I never got around to that. But I used to talk now and then."

The host thought for a long time. "I hope you won't be offended," he said finally. "But we've got to face facts in Gold Beach. Are You Jewish?"

"Yes," He smiled.

The host wheezed unhappily. "We were counting on You being an extra man at dinner at the Wampum. But, I'm sorry, it can't be done. There's a rule, see? Don't blame me, I didn't make it. If I bring You, and they find out, I'll be asked to resign from the club. It's the oldest and best club around here, and we've got to live here, see?"

The host's wife hovered impatiently over them. "We're late, Horace," she said. "Tell your friend good-bye. You know how they are at the club about holding tables, especially on Christmas Eve."

The guests crowded out on the curb and piled into their convertibles and limousines. The host stayed behind, momentarily and put his arm around the Stranger's shoulders.

"No hard feelings?" the man asked.

"No hard feelings," He answered warmly.

Then He was alone in the now-darkened street. The air was tender in the palms. They reminded Him of the palms He had known as a Child, and the palms he had known for one brief Sunday, as a Man.

"Well, a little more time," He sighed. Then He clapped on His new hat, looked up at the star-studded heavens and cupped His hands around his sensitive mouth.

"Michael!" He shouted at the top of His lungs. "Oh, Michael!"

It is obvious that Bob Considine, the award-winning King Features reporter, commentator and lecturer, was tapped by the Big Editor to laugh our enemies out of space. All bigots are enemies of society. "Where the enemy shall come in like a flood . . . The spirit of the Lord shall lift up a standard against Him." (Isaiah 59:19)

Georgie Jessel told me he once took a young black girl into the Waldorf-Astoria dining room. This was when we were still colorblind. The maitre d' stopped them at the door. "Who made the reservation?" he asked coldly.

"Abraham Lincoln," Jessel answered.

You've got to laugh at the haters—and they are laughable. Groucho Marx was with his wife and daughter when they passed a beautiful swimming pool. It was a very hot Sunday afternoon and they decided to take a dip. The manager was sorry, "but this place is restricted."

"That's okay," Groucho flattened him. "I'm Jewish and my wife's Gentile. That makes my daughter half Jewish. Do you mind if she goes in the water up to her waist?"

A friend of mine was in Toronto and found himself at a United Jewish Appeal dinner. The man sitting next to him was a Rabbi. "What is your name?" the cleric wanted to know. "Joe Cohen," was the answer.

"Mr. Cohen," the rabbi said, "you're a Jew. You should be proud you're a Jew. We have 80,000 Jews here in Toronto—and not one Jew is in jail."

"Why," asked Joe, "is it restricted?"

Dick Gregory walked into a restaurant in the South and sat down at a front table. "I'm sorry," the waitress said, "we don't serve Negroes."

"That's okay," he answered, "I don't eat 'em. I'll have some fried chicken."

Two ladies from Brooklyn were discussing the decision of the Ecumenical Congress.

"Did you hear that the high Catholics decided that the Jews were not responsible for the crucifixion of Jesus?" Mrs. Traum said.

"So," asked Mrs. De May, "who, then, is responsible?"

"I'm not sure," said Mrs. Traum. "I think they suspect the Puerto Ricans."

The black gentleman sat at a counter in a kosher restaurant trying to figure out the menu: Gefilte fish, Kreplach soup, Stuffed cabbage, Kishkah. "Say," he asked the counterman, "you got any chitlins?"

"Do I got what?"

"Forget it. Bring me a plate of hominy grits."

"We ain't got it."

"Okay, then I'll have some pig's knuckles."

"Pigs—in here?"

"Jees," the black man barked, "it'll be a lifetime before this joint is ready for integration."

Laughter brings bigotry into the light and exposes it for the evil that it is.

"For every one that doeth evil hateth the light, neither

164

cometh to the light, lest his deeds should be reproved." (John 3:20)

No matter how much steam is built up in oppression, there is always one small safety valve—humor. Whether the villain is Pharaoh, Caesar, Hitler, Pontius Pilate, or your local butcher, laughter can be your shield—but faith is your rock.

Perhaps the unique ingredient of our enduring faith is a man's capacity to laugh at himself for "a merry heart doeth good like a medicine." (Proverbs 17:22)

Jean Stapleton plays the part of Edith, the dingbat wife of Archie Bunker in "All In The Family." In real life, Jean is a dedicated and devoted student of the Bible. A God-fearing, God-loving lady who lives by the Good Book.

"Archie's a bigot—a superbigot," Miss Stapleton says, "and we get most of our laughs from his outrageous points of view, his rantings against other races, and almost anything new or strange to him. If it's true that the bravest man who ever lived was the first fellow to eat an oyster, you have some idea of where Archie would rate for courage—and how he'd camouflage his fear with a loud tirade."

By being extreme, and therefore ridiculous and funny to us, Archie has made millions of people aware of the absurdity of bias, bigotry and intolerance of any kind.

Prejudice can floor you in a million different ways, if you are not able to recognize it and laugh it out of existence. Prejudice is expensive—expensive because of its great cost on our daily lives. Prejudice is the enemy of mankind and only you have the power to erase it. "Behold, I give unto you power to tread on serpents and scorpions, and over all the power of the enemy: and nothing shall by any means hurt you." (Luke 10:19)

How often have you heard them say: "All colored people smell," "Jews have horns," "He's Italian—he must be in the Mafia," "That dumb Polack." You hear it on the subway, in your office, on the television: "The male chauvinist pig," or "She's a women's libber—she must be a lesbian," or "Hard hats are all fascists," or "If he's got a beard he must be a Commie."

All show people are immoral—ballet dancers are homosexuals—longhairs don't bathe—cabdrivers are bums—he's a square, he won't smoke pot—she's faithful to her husband, she must be frigid—what does he know, he's too young?—what does he know, he's too old?—cops are pigs—all Puerto Ricans are lazy, the Irish are drunks, the British are cold, the French are arrogant, the Germans are dogmatic, the Scots are cheap.

That's what "they" say. Who are "they?" They are the Archie Bunkers of the world who feel that if you repeat a lie often enough, sooner or later everybody will believe it.

Well, we've got to know the truth. "Ye shall know the truth, and the truth shall make you free." (John 8:32) And it shall free "them" too. "But if ye have bitter envying and strife in your hearts, glory not, and lie not against the truth." (James 3:14)

The truth is that most prejudice is caused by envy, jealousy, or lack of talent. "They" are the ones who start the lies. I know a stutterer who applied for a job as a radio announcer. When he was turned down he cried, "T-t-those b-b-bums, th-th-they t-t-turned me d-d-down because th-th-they're anti-anti-S-s-s-semitic."

Or the poor-soul comic who insisted that the night club was run by the Mafia because he used dirty language, laid a bomb, and was canceled opening night.

Every critic is a fag when you're a loser. The girl who didn't get the part says the one who did is sleeping with the producer.

The answer is found in my friend Isaiah (54:17): "No weapon that is formed against thee shall prosper; and every tongue that shall rise against thee in judgment thou shalt condemn. This is the heritage of the servants of the Lord, and their righteousness is of me, saith the Lord."

I guess all of us are guilty of some prejudice at one time in our lives. Even the loving Jean Stapleton admits that she didn't like calves' liver when she was a little girl. She would rather go hungry than eat it—and often did.

"The interesting thing," says Jean, "I never even tasted

calves' liver until I was an adult. I simply disliked the looks of it and knew that I would despise it. Today I adore calves' liver."

I'm sure Archie Bunker hates calves' liver.

"As for me," Miss Stapleton says, "I have seen my own personal prejudgments rob me of pleasure and peace of mind.

"Of course, I have tried to cure these prejudices and I recall one time in particular when a conscious effort at healing resulted in a crucial breakthrough in my acting career."

It happened when Jean wanted a part in a show so badly, she was out of her mind when she didn't get it. She had to do something about this "injustice."

"In those days," Jean says, "as well as today, I had my own way of finding help when needed. I took out my Bible. After all, I had been going to Sunday-School classes in our church since the age of two. And I also took out my concordance, that remarkable compilation of all the key words in the Bible and where they appear. I flipped through the pages of the concordance to the 'J's,' mumbling theatrically all the while, 'Justice is what I need, justice . . .' But before I could find 'justice' my eyes fell on 'judge.'

" 'For the Lord is our Judge.' (Isaiah 33:22.)

"I picked up the Bible and sped to Isaiah. I had explored scripture in this fashion many times before, sometimes losing myself for hours in random adventure. Now, chapter 33 . . . There was: 'For the Lord is our Judge, the Lord is our lawgiver, the Lord is our King; He will save us.'

"What was this I was asking about justice? Should I pray about this and try leaving justice to the Lord?

"I prayed; I relinquished the matter to the Highest Power. My anger disappeared. One day soon after, the director called me and offered me the part. Not only that, but an important agent saw me in the show and offered me an important part in *Harvey*—and I was on my way.

"Today, when I get emotional about something I think somebody has done to me, I try to think back to that experience before I start hurling a few hasty, bigoted thunderbolts. I recall that I never succeeded in changing the director's opinion of me; nor did I change my own opinion. I had simply left the judging to the Lawgiver, and He decided for both of us."

Jean treasures a sermon entitled, "God and Archie Bunker," written by the pastor of the Brentwood Presbyterian Church in California. In that sermon, Dr. Spencer Marsh, Jr., noted Archie's self-centeredness, his cliché-ridden bravado, his imprisonment inside his own narrow opinions. He quoted some dialogue from the show, from the night Archie was talking to his son-in-law, saying, "I've been making my way in the world for a long time, sonny boy, and one thing I know—a man better watch out for number one. It's the survival of the fittest."

Dr. Marsh said that Archie is out of position, that Archie is a mixed-up person, "because the number-one slot which he claims, is reserved for God." He sees Archie as the elder brother in Christ's prodigal son parable, the one who stands outside the house grumbling about his rights while the welcome-home party is going on inside. The walls that separate him from the party are self-imposed, self-righteous, judgmental ones.

"That's one reason," Jean Stapleton says, "I worry about prejudice. It could keep me from the party. It could keep me from enjoying the company of other people and what they have to offer, just as surely as it almost kept me from the simple pleasure of calves' liver or, more important, the big break of my career.

"And poor Archie, like a lot of us, never listens, never learns. He'll never know that by blindly pushing away the oyster, he might be missing the pearl."

Carroll O'Connor believes that the best way to exorcise bigotry is to bring it out in the open. By portraying Archie Bunker as a loser who is defeated by his own stubborn refusal to face up to present-day realities, O'Connor demonstrates the futility of Bunker's archaic attitudes.

In the make-believe world of TV, Archie Bunker is not only a White Anglo-Saxon Protestant, but America's crankiest conservative—the word should be "retarded." He's so right he thinks the Birch Society is a bunch of Commies. But in real life, Carroll O'Connor, who became a star playing the cantankerous, self-rightous working-class bigot, is an Irish Catholic with astonishingly liberal views.

"Bigotry is a trap," says Carroll. "Take anti-Semitism. Children are thrown into that trap at an early age. The child first hears about anti-Semitism when he is about six. Parents tell him he can't play with certain children or make disparaging remarks about kids, suggesting that there's something sinister about Jews.

"A child at that age believes anything his parents tell him because such biases are invisible to the child since they are planted in a climate of family love. It's a loving mother or father who misleads him. So the innocent child is in a trap encased in love."

It's hard to dispel a parental idea. The tendency is to accept it. It's gospel. The child becomes an adult with the firm belief that the Jew is to be avoided as an enemy. O'Connor says, "Considering how the child has bias laid upon him by his parents or sometimes society itself, you've got to forgive him because it's not his fault."

Another trap inherited by the white American is his prejudice toward the blacks. "People like Archie," Carroll says, "are made to believe that there is something inferior in the black, that there is even a danger in touching the black with your hands. I remember some little kids I knew thinking that any really close, intimate contact with black people would result in bad health and perhaps death. That wasn't in the South; that was in New York."

O'Connor feels that our prejudice toward the black is smuggled in during our formative years side by side with parental love. One doesn't want to say, "My mother was all wrong," so the growing child goes on with Mother's ideas—out of love.

O'Connor feels that one good way of getting rid of all the bigotry is "to look squarely at it." He agrees with those who say that the show is bringing many of the unexpressed American fears and biases out into broad daylight and then, one by one,

169

lampooning them and thus setting society free of them. "I believe" says Carroll, "it's not the black man or the Pole or the Catholic who is put down by the show's ethnic humor so much as society's silly, exaggerated fears and biases."

Satire has always been a dramatic device for exposing the faults of any given society. Getting laughs at their expense is a sure way of reforming the sinner. "I never would have taken the role of Archie Bunker," Carroll told me, "if I didn't believe in its possibility for good."

O'Connor says: "In 'All in the Family,' we try to present a truthful situation where a man's faults can be seen and judged by viewers without any comment being needed from the creators. I think we get as close to the truth as we possibly can, and I think I succeed with Archie in getting very close to a real character. We show a man making fundamental moral errors. If people see a truthful situation and a truthful character, and the life that is shown is an erroneous life, something has to be learned. Everybody laughs at Archie. But nobody would like to live with Archie or even have Archie as a neighbor."

The man who plays America's most celebrated bigot thinks that Archie Bunker needs help. And a good way to cleanse society of bigotry, he believes, is to look at it squarely, satirize it and hopefully laugh it out of existence.

Father Jack Wintz, O.F.M., of the *St. Anthony Messenger*, asked Carroll O'Connor "if there is any hope for Archie Bunker, who represents the trapped American and, in some way, even the self-righteous American."

Father Wintz wanted to know, "Can Archie Bunker be saved?"

"He can't do it himself," O'Connor answered. "If Archie is to be saved, he needs help from many sources—from the media, television, the press, the education system and special leadership from the Catholic Church—in fact, from all churches. They all must play a part in Archie's healing. All the churches have to help this man—and they have to speak very frankly to him, and they must take the risks involved in speaking frankly."

Father Wintz says, "Archie needs to be spoken to, healed and enlightened because Archie is a man who is having a sour life, who comes home every day mad at the world—and whose inability to get joy out of life is due to his fundamental errors. Don't hate him—feel sorry for him—and his errors."

O'Connor says, "We have to forgive Archie because his basic errors are things he inherited unconsciously. Everybody has to be forgiving. Christ forgives, we must forgive too. We have to forgive instead of calling for vengeance, instead of harboring smug dislikes, hatred and contempt. But of course we don't need such preachments; we all know this.

"Probably Archie Bunker knows this too; but I am now speaking of a knowledge that we sometimes call grace, a light that glows dimly in Archie. How to make it burn brightly? Pray for the man—and put a trust and hope in mysterious developments."

For nearly a century major-league baseball had excluded the black man. Jackie Robinson, with an assist from Branch Rickey—and a close call from The Umpire, proved that a champion is a champion, black or white. Jackie helped the Brooklyn Dodgers win a pennant his first year in the big-time. But he also cherished another triumph. Baseball as a whole had come to accept the Negro. From then on, the black ballplayer, to make the grade, simply had to be a good enough player— no matter his color.

"It wasn't a question so much of a black athlete making good as a big-leaguer," Jackie told me later, "but whether the whole racial question would be advanced or retarded.

"I prayed as I never had before . . .

"It all started when Branch Rickey, president of the Brooklyn Dodgers, asked me to join his baseball organization. I was to be the first black man to play in organized baseball— that is, if I were good enough to make the grade.

"I'll never forget that opening scene. Mr. Rickey's office was large and well furnished. But all I could see were the four pictures on the wall. One was of Leo Durocher, who was the manager of the Dodgers, another was Charlie Barrett, the baseball scout, the third was General Chennault, and the fourth and largest smiled down on me with calm reassurance, the portrait of the sad, trusting Abraham Lincoln who had pleaded for malice toward none . . .

"Mr. Rickey," Jackie said, "it's like a dream come true—for me—for my race. For almost a century there has been racial exclusion in Ivy-League baseball. There will be trouble ahead—for you, for me, for my people, and for baseball."

Rickey was only beautiful. "How can any trouble stand up to the Power behind us," he said. "God is with us in this, Jackie. You know your Bible. It's good, simple Christianity for us to face realities and to recognize what we're up against. We can't go out and preach and crusade and beat our heads against a wall. We've got to fight out our problems together with tact and common sense."

To give him experience and seasoning, Mr. Rickey sent Jackie to play with the Montreal Royals, a farm club for the Dodgers. Of course, there was trouble right from the start. But they were ready for it. Preseason exhibition games were canceled because of "mixed athletes," although the official reason was always different.

"Some of my teammates may have resented me," Jackie told me. "If so, I didn't blame them. They had enough problems playing ball without being part of a racial issue. I tried hard not to develop 'rabbit ears,' a malady picked up by all athletes who are sensitive to abuse and criticism, shouted from the fans."

Jackie's opening game for Montreal was the greatest. Nervous as he was and with all that pressure, he still knocked out four hits—including a home run.

"But as the season went on," Jackie said, "my play grew erratic. I was trying too hard. I knew I had to keep my temper bridled at every turn. Guarding so carefully against outbursts can put a damper on your competitive spirit.

"Every athlete likes to blow his top once in a whole—over a bad decision or being heckled from the opposing bench. But I didn't dare let loose this way. Many would have branded me a 'hothead' and point to my outburst as a reason why Negroes should not play in organized baseball. This was one of the hardest problems I had to face."

It was worth it for Jackie. That year he helped Montreal with the Junior World Series. And he won the batting championship of the league with an average of .349. He was credited with the most hits and the most prayers.

"On April 10, 1947, Branch Rickey made the announcement that gave me my greatest thrill," Jackie told me. "I was to join the Brooklyn Dodgers and become the first Negro to compete in the major leagues.

"It was Montreal all over again—only this time the pressure was much greater, the competition keener, and the stakes tremendous.

"Again I faced the same problems. An opposing player drove a hard grounder to the infield. When he crossed first base, his spikes bit painfully into my foot. Accident or deliberate? Who can tell? But the first reaction of a competitive ballplayer is to double up fists and lash out. I saw a blinding red. It took every bit of my discipline to bridle my temper. But when my teammates rushed to my support in white-hot anger, it gave me the warmest feeling I've ever felt. At that moment I belonged—and that went for every black man in baseball from there on."

"Where does all the credit go?" I asked Jackie.

"To God—to prayer," he answered. "I'll never forget what Branch Rickey said to me that very first day! 'God is with us in this, Jackie.' And he sure was."

"What shall we then say to these things?—if God be for us, who can be against us?" (Romans 8:31)

Hank Aaron was only fourteen years old when Jackie Robinson became the first black to play in the big leagues. "I guess if I had real hero-worship for anyone, it could be for Jackie Robinson of the Brooklyn Dodgers," Hank says. "I read everything I could find about him. What fascinated me so much was that Jackie was an emotional, explosive kind of ballplayer. Yet during that crucial first year in the big leagues, he didn't lose his temper once, in spite of a steady barrage of insults from fans and other players.

"How did he keep control? I learned later that he prayed a lot for help. And he also had a sense of destiny about what he was doing, so much so that he felt God's presence with him. He learned to put aside his pride and his quick temper for the bigger things he was doing."

It's Jackie Robinson's example, his prayers and his working with the Manager Upstairs, that made it possible for "me, Hank Aaron, a nobody from Mobile, Alabama, to challenge the home-run record of the great Babe Ruth.

"It's Jackie's example that helped me when I faced a similar situation while playing in Jacksonville, Florida, in the Southern Association back in 1953. Blacks had never played in this league before. Three of us—Horace Garner, Felix Mantella and myself—were the ones to break the color line.

"I'm not the crusader type, and there were times, frankly, when I wanted out. Like those bus trips from the ballpark after each game on the road. The white players were left at the hotel while Horace, Felix and I were taken to a private home.

"The best way to lick this racial thing is to play well. Play so well that the fans forget your color." And that's what happened that year. As one sports writer put it, "Aaron led the league in everything but hotel accommodations."

Like Jackie, Hank decided to set aside the things that bugged him to get on to bigger and better things for him and his team and his race. "There will always be people who resent you if you try to climb too high," Hank told us, "but I also know this; I need to depend on Someone who is bigger, stronger and wiser than I am. I can't do it alone. God is my strength. He gave me a body and some talent and the freedom to develop it. He helps me when things go wrong. He forgives me when I fall on my face. He lights the way.

"The Lord willing, I'll set a new home-run record. If I don't, that's okay, too. I've had a wonderful time in baseball and have enough memories to last two lifetimes. I have been blessed."

174

Jackie and Hank have always led the league in prayers and have proven to all of baseball, white and black, Jew and Christian, that you can't make it out there alone. It's not unusual to hear the Met's greatest pitching ace, Tug McGraw, holler from the dugout, "You gotta believe.

"When I'm in a slump," Tug told me, "I know it's only loss of confidence. My arm is okay, my body is fine, so I gotta believe in my God-given talent. All I do is look up and ask, 'What gives, God?' *He* gives. You gotta Believe."

Ron Swoboda told me that he believes in the hereafter. "I know there's a report card on me and He's going to watch those marks when I get up there. So I use the talent He gave me for good—and I can't lose."

Monte Irvin, the famous Hall-of-Famer of the New York Giants, now Assistant Commissioner of Baseball, is another example of faith in action. "What do you *think* I was doing on my knees in the batter's circle?" Monte exclaimed. "I was praying to the Big Boss. 'Please God, if it's your will, I need a base hit—if not for me, then do it for my daughter Patti, and please, God, if you can't do it this time, I'll understand.' I talked to Him, too, whenever we were in trouble—for some of the other guys—it's what led the Giants to the pennant that year."

The confidence that Tug, Monte, Hank, Ron and Jackie talked about, had to come from only *one* source—and Willie Mays was loaded with it. I was having lunch with him just before he joined the Mets. He was holding out for something like $150,000 a year. "I think you're the greatest," I said. "But, Willie, that's a lot of loot. Richard Nixon, the President of the United States, doesn't get that much money." He looked at me and smiled. "Yeah, but Mr. Nixon didn't have as good a year as I did."

Prejudice is not reserved for black ballplayers or Jewish comedians or Puerto Rican laborers. It can attack rich man, poor man, beggar man—or even the President of the United States.

Prejudice is a disease that can be wiped out only by giving it a lot of air. That's just what John F. Kennedy did when he was challenged by a group of religious leaders who wanted to know if a Roman Catholic President could be loyal to his oath of office and to his church at the same time.

JFK's answer was heard around the world.

Because I am a Catholic, and no Catholic has ever been elected President, it is apparently necessary for me to state once again—not what kind of Church I believe in, for that should be important only to me, but what kind of United States of America I believe in.

I believe in an America where the separation of Church and State is absolute—where no Catholic prelate could tell the President (should he be a Catholic) how to act and no Protestant minister would tell his parishioners for whom to vote. . . .

I believe in America where no religious body seeks to impose its will directly or indirectly upon the general populace or the public acts of its officials—and where religious liberty is so indivisible that an act against one church is treated as an act against all.

For while this year it may be a Catholic against whom the finger of suspicion is pointed, in other years it has been, and may someday be again, a Jew—or a Quaker—or a Unitarian—or a Baptist. It was Virginia's harassment of Baptist preachers, for example, that led to Jefferson's statute of religious freedom. Today, I may be the victim—but tomorrow it may be you, until the whole fabric of our harmonious society is ripped apart at a time of great national peril. . . .

I am not the Catholic candidate for President. I am the Democratic party's candidate for President, who happens to be Catholic. . . . I do not intend to disavow either my views or my church in order to win this election.

But if this election is decided on the basis that forty million Americans lost their chance of being President on the day they were baptized, then it is the whole nation that will be the loser in the eyes of Catholics and non-Catholics around the world, in the eyes of history, and in the eyes of our own people. . . .

176

Chapter 16.

A Dose of Joy Is a Spiritual Cure

There are so many headaches in the world today—if Moses would come down from Mount Sinai now, the tablets he would carry would be aspirin.

That's why God gave us a sense of humor—to turn tragedy into joy. And a dose of joy is a spiritual cure.

Humor is a divine quality, and God has the greatest sense of humor of all. He must have, or he couldn't have made so many politicians.

Some of the greatest believers and Bible-thumpers have given me the most irreverent but respectful laughs when they get on the religious kick—and I'm going to try to pass them on to you.

And remember, it is more blessed to give than to receive. Besides, you don't have to write thank-you notes.

Bob Hope figures he was put on this earth to glorify the Lord by spreading joy, and he doesn't care who he smears with it. "I am the first to tell you my wife is a good Catholic," Bob says. "We can't get insurance—too many candles in the house. Do you know our grocery bills are astronomical? Three thousand a week—fifty for food, the rest for candles."

Bob never refuses to do any Catholic benefit. He did once, and it snowed in his living room for three days—in Miami—during the summer.

I remember at one dinner he neglected to introduce Cardinal Cooke. "He told me he forgave me," Bob told me later, "but I noticed I haven't won a bingo game since."

Of course, Hope helps all religions. I just read where he gave a huge donation to Southern Methodist University. I guess Bob knows he can't take it with him, so he's sending it ahead.

These offerings come in assorted shapes, sizes and religions. Use them any time. Just not when the service is on. We all know the Lord has a sense of humor—but let's not push Him too far.

Sam Burns, a Southern Negro, was refused entrance in a "white" church. The sexton told him to go to his own church and pray to God and he will feel much better.

The next Sunday he was back again. "Don't get upset," he said to the sexton. "I'm not forcing my way in. I just came to tell you that I took your advice and it came out just fine. I prayed to God and He told me, 'Don't feel bad about it, Sam. I've been trying to get into that church for years and I haven't made it yet!'"

This lady wanted to mail a Bible to her son at college. The post office clerk wanted to know if the package contained anything breakable—"Only the Ten Commandments."

Union officials have only one thing against God—He worked a six-day week.

St. Peter and St. Thomas were playing golf. St. Thomas's first drive on a 600-yard hole was a hole-in-one.

St. Peter got a bit irritated. "Okay, Tom," he said, "let's knock off the miracles and play golf."

180

The minister was discussing with some of the businessmen of his parish what it must be like in Heaven. "One thing you can be sure of," the man of the cloth noted, "we will have a good rest up there. No buying or selling is conducted in Heaven."

"Of course not," one man interrupted, "that's not where business has gone."

Would you say a monastery is a home for unwed fathers?

I love the attitude of my good friend Father Bob: "Since I believe in the Bible, I'm sure there is a hell. But I also believe in God's mercy—and therefore I'm sure it's empty."

An elderly Irish gentleman was on his deathbed. His priest asked him if he had renounced the devil.

"Just a minute, now, Father," he replied. "Sure now, I don't think this is a good time to be making enemies."

All the trouble started in the Garden of Eden when Eve bit into a piece of fruit. It was nothing compared to the trouble I had when I did the same thing in Mexico.

Do you think the Three Wise Men are the guys who got out of the stock market at the right time?

An optimist is a man who goes to the window in the morning and says, "Good morning, God!" A pessimist says, "Good God—morning!"

The town was new to the traveling preacher and he wanted to find the post office. He asked one of the boys standing on the corner for directions. The young man showed him the way. The preacher thanked him and added, "You're a very bright and courteous young lad. How would you like to come and listen to my sermon this evening so that I may show you the way to heaven?"

"You're gonna show me the way to heaven?" the boy said. "Why, you don't even know the way to the post office."

A Jewish boy and a Catholic boy were arguing. "My priest knows more than your rabbi," the Catholic boy challenged.

"Why not? You tell him everything."

Father Bob Perella, the show-biz priest, welcomes suggestions from his parishioners. One neighborhood enthusiast came in with this suggestion: "Why don't we have a drive-in confessional with a huge red and green neon sign reading: 'Stop and Tell or Go to Hell!' "

Jewish temples and synagogues do not pass the plate as do the Christian churches. Consequently, they have to raise money in other ways. One of them is the sale of tickets for reserved seats for the High Holy Days when business is best.

On one holiday, a young man went to the synagogue in Philadelphia to look for his uncle. The guard refused him admittance because he had no ticket.

"Look, pal," the youngster said, "I gotta see my uncle— it's very important."

"Not a chance," said the guard. "Everybody says that. Nobody gets in here without a ticket."

"But," the boy pleaded, "it's a matter of life and death— please—I'll only be two minutes."

"Well, okay, if it's so important," the guard said. "But don't let me catch you praying."

One young man I know recently quit the Jewish faith to become a Catholic priest. Now his mother introduces him as, "My son, the Father."

The six-year-old son of a Protestant minister and his little Catholic girlfriend from the next block fell in the lake with their clothes on and had to take all their clothes off to dry in the sun. The boy came running to his father and announced with glee, "Well, now at last I understand the difference between Protestants and Catholics."

The two gay boys said to Noah: "You said two of every kind."

It happened in the Garden of Eden.
"Do you really love me?" Eve asked Adam.
"Who else?"

The lady and her small son were swimming in the surf and there was a very heavy undertow. She was holding her son tightly by the hand and they were splashing around happily when a huge wall of water loomed up ahead of them. As they watched in horror, this tidal wave rose higher and higher directly in front of them and crashed over them. When the water receded the little boy was nowhere to be found. Panic-stricken, the mother searched in the water screaming, "Melvin . . . Melvin . . . Where are you, Melvin?" When it was obvious the child was lost, washed out to sea, the distraught mother lifted her eyes to Heaven and prayed, "Oh, dear and merciful Father, please . . . please . . . take pity on me and return my beautiful child. I will promise eternal gratitude to You. I promise I'll never cheat on my husband again. I'll never cheat on my income tax again. I'll be kind to my mother-in-law. I'll give up smoking . . . Anything . . . anything . . . only please grant me this one favor and return my son." Just then another wall of water loomed up and crashed over her head. When the water receded there was her small son standing there. She clasped him to her bosom, kissed him, clung to him, then she looked at him a moment and, once again, turned her eyes heavenward. Looking up, she said, "But he had a hat."

A Catholic priest and a Protestant minister had an argument over their respective faiths. As they parted the priest said, "Let us go our separate ways. You continue to worship the Lord in your way, and I will continue to worship Him in His."

I went to one Catholic dinner. I knew it was one of theirs. I left my car in front of the hotel and they raffled it off.

Bishop Fulton J. Sheen, who was equally at home in front of the TV cameras and in the pulpit, was listening to all the television stars accepting their awards. Each thanked his writer for making it all possible.

When the Bishop received his award he stepped up to the microphone and said graciously, "I also want to pay tribute to my writers—Mathew, Mark, Luke and John."

Will Rogers offered this interesting observation: "A Christian should so live that he would not be afraid to sell the family parrot to the town gossip."

A Catholic girl and a Jewish boy fell madly in love. But their religious beliefs interfered. The Irish Catholic mother advised her daughter, "Sell him a bill of goods. Teach him the beauty and joys of Catholicism. Make him a Catholic." The girl did. She sold him and sold him and the wedding date was set. One day before the marriage the girl came home and sobbed, "The marriage is off."

"Why?" the mother asked. "Didn't you sell him?"

"I think I oversold him. Now he wants to be a Priest."

The Jew and the Christian were having a heated argument. "Your whole religion is based on ours," the Jewish gentleman insisted. "You even took the Ten Commandments from us."

"True," said the Christian. "We may have taken them—but you certainly can't say we've kept them."

Father Bob, the show-business priest, was always against it—but now he thinks that priests should marry.

"Why the change of mind?" I asked.

"Oh," he answered, "there are a couple of Monsignors I'd like to stick with mothers-in-law."

184

Pope John said it: "When the body gets worn out, the soul gets in shape."

"Vicar, didn't you always tell me that the Bible says it's wrong to profit from other people's mistakes?"

"Yes, that's right."

"In that case, how about giving me back the twenty dollars I paid you for marrying us last month."

Four men of the cloth were having a confidential talk and discussing their vices.

"I like pork," the rabbi admitted.

"I drink a bottle of bourbon a day," said the Protestant minister.

"I have a girlfriend on the side," confessed the priest.

They all turned to the Baptist minister who shrugged. "Me? I like to gossip."

Pope John liked to reminisce about his peasant origins. "In Italy there are three ways of losing money," he enjoyed saying, "women, gambling and farming. My father chose the most boring of the three."

My favorite priest story is of the father who was stopped by a cop for speeding and declared, "I'm Father Fox." The officer wasn't too impressed and growled, "I don't care if you're Mother Goose. You're getting a ticket."

The two nuns were enjoying the baseball game when one of the shrimps in back of them growled to his friend, "You can't see a thing. These nuns' hats are blocking the whole game. Remind me to move to Cleveland where only ten percent of the people are Catholics."

"Better still, let's go to Omaha," his friend answered, "where only five percent are Catholic."

"I've got a better idea," one of the nuns said. "Why don't you both go to hell where you will find *no* Catholics."

185

Father Bob was having dinner at Danny's with Rabbi Mann. "Come on," said Father Bob, "when are you gonna let yourself go and have some bacon or ham?"

"At your wedding," said the rabbi.

The two youngsters saw the Protestant minister walking down the street. "Who's that Father?" one kid asked. "He's no Father," said the other, "he's got four kids."

The very religious Quaker heard a noise in his house and when he investigated he discovered a burglar. He went for his gun and stood quietly in the doorway pointing at the robber. "Friend," he said softly, "I would do thee no harm, but thou standest where I am about to shoot."

The preacher was telling his clan that there are over seven-hundred different kinds of sin. He was besieged with mail and phone calls the next day from people who wanted the list —to make sure they weren't missing anything.

Peter the Fisherman was stopped by a bunch of hoodlums on the corner. "Is it true that your Master tells you to turn the other cheek? Is that in the Bible?" the head of the riffraff asked.

"Yes," said Peter quietly.

"Well, here's a slap on the kisser. Now how about the other cheek?" When he slapped Peter the second time, on the other cheek, he smirked, "and here's another." As he lifted his hand for the third time, Peter picked him up and threw him over the fence.

"It also says in the Bible," Peter reminded them, " 'Thou shall not tempt the Lord.' "

He'll never change his religion—he thinks he's God.

And Billy Graham has the topper: "The smallest package I ever saw was a man wrapped up wholly in himself."

Was it Benjamin Franklin who said: "God heals—and the doctor takes the fees."

Alan King: "Anyway—the priests so far have the lowest divorce rate."

"I don't know if God exists," said one university professor, "but with what's going on in our colleges today, it would be better for His reputation if He didn't."

When the old man came to see his son in America, he was shocked to find that the young man did not follow the Jewish laws. "You mean," he asked, "you don't keep the dietary laws?"

"Papa, I eat in restaurants, and it's not easy to keep kosher."

"Do you keep the Sabbath, at least?"

"Sorry, papa, it's tough in America to do that."

"Tell me, son," the old man sneered, "are you still circumcised?"

I really hope you enjoyed these jokes. Mark Twain said, "The human race has only one effective weapon and that is laughter." Fred Allen said, "It is bad to suppress laughter—it goes back down and spreads your hips."

Ken Murray said, "God's greatest gift to man is the joy of laughter. We laugh before we speak. We laugh before we walk."

An onion can make people cry, but there has never been a vegetable to make you laugh—and don't go calling me a vegetable.

My only wish right now is that I was Adam, instead of Adams—then nobody could say about any of these jokes: "I heard them before."

Chapter 17.

All Roads Lead to God

All roads lead to God. If you believe, there are no dead-end streets.

It doesn't matter if you are Catholic, Protestant, Jew or come-as-you-are believer. If you are looking for God, He will build a path to your door and personally take you all the way.

There are many different roads to the mountaintop. All lead to God—joy—truth and love—and what more can you expect unless you're evil-minded.

At the All-Faith chapel in New York City is to be found an affirmation of the master truths of the major religions of the world:

Christianity: "Thou shalt love the Lord thy God with all thine heart . . . and thy neighbor as thyself."

Judaism: "Behold how good and pleasant it is for brethren to dwell together in unity."

Hinduism: "Truth is one: sages call it by various names. . . . Various are the ways that lead to God."

Islam: "No one of you is a believer until he loves for his brother what he loves for himself."

Confucianism: "The broad-minded see the truth in different religions; the narrow-minded see only the differences."

Zoroastrianism: "Whatever road we take joins the highway that leads to the Eternal One."

Shinto: Sincerity is a single virtue binding God and man in one.

Buddhism: "Hold fast to the truth as a lamp. Seek salvation only in the truth . . . the truth hath been manifested in many ways." "For hatred does not cease by hatred. Hatred ceases by love."

Every religion gives truth top billing. "Ye shall know the truth—and the truth shall set you free." Everybody is always asking what is truth.

Some say it's the Ten Commandments. Others declare: "Be ye therefore perfect even as your Father which is in heaven is perfect." (Matthew 5:48) There are those who claim the truth by knowing that God is all: "If thou canst believe . . . all things are possible to him that believeth." (Mark 9:23)

Almost all accept the Lord's Prayer as the Truth:

> Our Father which art in heaven, hallowed be thy name. Thy kingdom come. Thy will be done in Earth, as it is in heaven. Give us this day our daily bread. And forgive us our debts, as we forgive our debtors. And lead us not into temptation, but deliver us from evil: For thine is the kingdom, and the power, and the glory, for ever. Amen. MATTHEW (6:9–13)

Anybody can find the Truth if they look for it hard enough and long enough. You never can tell where or when it will show up. The distinguished playwright, author, director, producer and lecturer, Dore Schary, found it at a dinner table. I'll let my friend Dore tell it to you exactly as he told it to me:

"I have very seldom examined my faith, but some years ago a casual experience gave me an opportunity to explore my basic feeling toward God. I was at a dinner party and was sitting to the right of a very wealthy lady whom I had known for quite some years. She was charming and intelligent and a delightful dinner companion. Our relationship over many years had always been pleasant and warm.

"The dinner conversation had flowed through the wide variety of subjects that are usually covered in such company. We had touched briefly on Vietnam and the threat of war; lightly brushed past the Academy Awards; settled for a few moments on high taxes; commented with no gain on smog in Los Angeles and the traffic jams in New York; rattled through some comments on the urban crisis that led us into the environment of the home and the importance of religious education—and that subject had then led us into a serious discussion about God and what we felt about Him and about prayer. For a few moments I spoke with the natural reticence one has in discussing such an intensely personal matter, and when I finished, my dinner companion, whom we shall call Mrs. Blank, looked at me intently and asked, 'Tell me—do you really believe in all of that?'

"Probably the simplicity and the evenness of the question was what disconcerted me, but there is no denying that I was disconcerted. The question gave me a vague sense of uneasiness, much as if someone had approached me and casually asked, 'Do you really believe that your father loves you?' I found myself staring into Mrs. Blank's face. I had the feeling that I was about to hear something very strange and terrible —that I was going to be told quickly and scientifically and irrevocably that such faith was a wasted thing.

"The added few seconds that I took to examine her question hung heavy and silent, and I was aware that the other eight persons at the table were looking at both Mrs. Blank and me. Then, finding my voice and my words, I asked Mrs. Blank, 'Do you believe in your money?'

"I had the ungentlemanly satisfaction of seeing the same expression on Mrs. Blank's face that I knew she had put upon mine. She then smiled and asked, 'What has my money got to do with it?' I suggested that it had a good deal to do with the matter. I knew that Mrs. Blank was worth many millions of dollars. I told her I had no idea how many millions she did have, but I wondered aloud if she had ever seen it or touched it or counted it. I assumed, and she agreed, that she had never really seen it or touched it or counted it.

I then asked Mrs. Blank how she knew she had the money. There were undoubtedly accountants' reports and business managers' files and lawyers' letters, but they were all pieces of paper—and someone might be cheating her or stealing from her. How was she really to know that the money was there in the bank or in the vault? How was she to know that the millions she counted on each day to sustain her life were actually there?

"Her assumption that the money existed was based on the fact that she could sit down and write a check for anything that crossed her mind—whether it was for furs or paintings or a car. She was expressing a faith that the money was there by writing checks for her food bills, gas and electricity and for the charities to which she gave generously. But how did she really know —how could she be sure—that all these checks would be honored? Simply because she believed they would be honored and she knew by experience and by faith that they would be.

"It occurred to me then that the faith I was talking about was much like having money in the bank. What I believed in was there, even though I had never seen it or touched it or counted it. I could always know that my grateful thanks for the wonderful things that have happened to me would be heard and accepted. In times of crisis I could draw on the account for patience and for hope. In times of anguish or unhappiness I could write a check for some peace of mind.

"The balances and the accounts and the statements that I get, I told Mrs. Blank, are all around me—the sun, the moon, the air, the beating of my heart, the joy of my family and my friends, the excitement of my work, and the countless other quiet proofs each day that God is here.

"Mrs. Blank heard me out, then said quietly, 'I'm afraid I have offended you.'

"I answered her truthfully, 'No, you haven't. As a matter of fact, you've given me the chance to state my faith in an arrangement of words that otherwise might never have occurred to me.'"

Like I have been saying, all roads lead to God. "Therefore I say unto you, what things soever ye desire, when ye pray, believe that ye receive them, and ye shall have them. (Mark 11:24)

What a wonderful opening to tell you the parable of the Pharisee and the publican. It certainly proves that the most effective praying is done in deep humility.

> Two men went up into the temples to pray; the one a Pharisee and the other a Publican.
>
> The Pharisee stood and prayed thus with himself, "God, I thank thee, that I am not as other men are, extortioners, unjust, adulterers, or even as this Publican. I fast twice a week, I give tithes of all that I possess."
>
> And the Publican, standing far off, would not lift up so much as his eyes unto heaven, but smote upon his breast, saying, "God, be merciful to me a sinner."
>
> I tell you, this man went down to his house justified rather than the other; for every one that exalteth himself shall be abased; and he that humbleth himself shall be exalted. (Luke 18:10–14)

What is truth? Truth is love. The Bible says time and time again and again. "Love ye one another—that is my commandment." The greatest story of this love happened in the closing days of World War II. A group of American prisoners in Europe showed their Nazi captors a sample of faith in action.

The rumor hit the prison camp that the Jewish soldiers among them were going to be separated from the others for "special treatment." All the guys in the camp were discussing it. The Jewish boys urged their buddies not to stick their necks out for them.

The next day when the command was given, "All prisoners of Jewish blood step forward," every single soldier stepped out!

All roads lead to God. Of course, there are a few detours here and there. In the case of Julia Meade there were some pretty good bumps along the way, "but if you know what you're going to find at the end of the road, it's sure worth it."

"I was ready to give up show business," the beautiful Julia Meade told me. "The bumps were pretty hard—I couldn't get a job—I was ready to open a candy store—or take up typing or get a job in a factory—anything to keep going—and then I decided to go to God."

"Just like that?" I asked.

"That's it," she explained. "I decided it's God's problem to work out. I decided to stop worrying about it and put the problem where it belongs." ('I speak not of myself—but the Father that dwelleth in me—he doeth the work.')

"Of course, I didn't say to God, You decide and decide *now*. I didn't give Him a deadline. I just said, 'Father, I thank Thee that Thou hast heard me. And I know that Thou hearest me always.' (John 11:41,42)

"And then I dropped it," she told me.

"You mean," I asked, "you didn't keep bugging Him?"

"The Bible says it good enough," Julia reminded me, 'but when ye pray, use no vain repetition, as the heathen do: for they think that they shall be heard for their much speaking. Be not ye therefore like unto them: for your Father knoweth what things ye have need of, before ye ask Him.' (Matthew 6:7,8)

"Some agent called me and offered me the Ed Sullivan Show. I never heard of this agent. He never heard of me. He told me later he had a tough time finding me but that somebody recommended me and he just couldn't remember who it was. I could have told him, but he wouldn't believe it. 'Father, I thank Thee—that Thou hast heard me.' "

"Say," I said, "God sure is magnanimous. Imagine using an agent as one of his angels."

Phyllis Diller's angel came in the person of Bob Hope. "I opened at this dump in Washington, D.C.," Phyllis told me. "I followed a line of sixty—some were even older—and laid a bomb that made the atomic one seem like a firecracker.

196

"I couldn't quit because I needed the money. Each night the egg I laid got bigger. I wanted to quit. Even kill myself. But how do you jump out of a basement window?

"One night my idol, Bob Hope, came in to see the show. I knew I had to make good—it was now or never. I couldn't blame the audience any more—or the chorus girls I followed —or the music—or the microphone. Bob Hope was out there —this was my chance—I couldn't blow this one.

"I pulled out every joke I knew. I used every trick. I sang, danced, gagged. That's when I started murdering myself: 'Everybody says I'm beautiful on the inside—leave it to me to be born inside-out . . . I went to a topless party—my upper plate fell out . . . Most people get a reservation at a beauty parlor— I was committed.'

"Would I lie to you? I was hilarious. I never was funnier or greater—and never laid a bigger bomb. I died like a dog.

"My only worry now was how do I sneak out without facing Bob Hope. I couldn't face anybody after this—especially my idol. I didn't even go to my dressing room. I figured I'd never come back again anyway. I'd go straight to the Potomac and jump in.

"Just as I was about to get into a cab, Hope put his hand on my shoulder, turned me around and said, 'You're great— I never enjoyed anything more in my life.' "

"But-but-but," I stammered, "there wasn't a laugh—or applause—or . . ."

" 'Don't worry about this audience—they eat their young in this town,' Bob said. 'I think you're funny. Of course, I also think Milton Berle is funny."

"It saved my life," Phyllis told me later, "and my career. Hope was the answer to my prayers. He was the angel God sent to put me back on the road."

What it did for Phyllis Diller is what we all need. Confidence—confidence in ourselves, and confidence in God who gives us the confidence in ourselves, sometimes through an angel we least expect.

That's why beautiful Phyllis Diller—inside and out—can deprecate herself to millions of watchers—because she knows

197

she's God's perfect child and He is watching over her always.

Now she can laugh when she says, "This dress I am wearing hides the Eighth Wonder of the World," or, "Look at this body—I'm the only female I know wears prescription underwear," or "I got my first laugh when my mother entered me in a baby contest."

Phyllis says, "Now when I tell these jokes, I tell them with confidence—because I've got the God power going for me."

Phyllis is overflowing with her gratitude to her Agent Upstairs who booked her in that dump in Washington because that's where His angel found her.

"God *is* the power," she says. "It isn't female, it isn't male, it has no gender. It is a power that *runs* the universe, and it is a good power. It is universal mind and consciousness. This power has always been there—has always been available to anyone who wishes to use it. All you have to do is—*plug in!*

"Electricity was always there as a power, but until we discovered it, and plugged in, and used it, we had no light. Plug in the God-power—have faith—think only good—talk only good—see only good—hear only good. That's God!"

Phyllis feels the three monkeys didn't go far enough. In addition to "see no evil," "hear no evil," and "speak no evil," there should be a fourth monkey: "think no evil."

When I told Phyllis I was going to write a book called *The God Bit,* she wanted to share her prayer with all of us. I put it down here with great love:

> ON THIS HAPPY DAY
> WE ARE THANKFUL FOR OUR BLESSINGS
> AND WE PRAY
> FOR RENEWED BELIEF
> IN OURSELVES
> AND EACH OTHER
> AND WE HOPE
> THIS BOND OF LOVE
> WILL EXPAND
> TO ENVELOP
> THE ENTIRE UNIVERSE.

Debbie Reynolds was put on the right road to God by her grandfather. "By a crazy coincidence," Debbie told me, "Grandpa and I were both born on April first. That's right—April Fools' Day. I guess that's the reason we were so close to each other.

"Grandpa loved the Bible and quoted from it so often that the men down at the railroad yard where he worked called him Preacher Harman. He had a quote to fit every occasion. Once, when we came upon an old farmer using the whip to his donkey, Grandpa raised his arm like a mighty apostle and said, "Remember what the Good Book says, 'Who soever harmeth a beast of the field, harmeth God—yea, even unto the lowly ass that straineth beneath his burden—Chronicles—eight–three.'

"Once, when two switchmen started fighting and throwing punches at each other, he said, 'Do not be fools—and they that live in friendship shall prosper and they that fall upon one another with blows shall reap only bruises for profit. Jeremiah —forty-six–twenty-four.'

"I have always believed that the Bible makes good sense and I was so impressed that when we got home I took down the Bible and looked up Jeremiah forty-six–twenty-four, but found nothing about friendship and bruises. Only a prophecy about Egypt and Babylon. The other quotes were not there either. That's when I realized that although Grandpa knew the Bible from the beginning to end, he only quoted for the good of others, especially if the good Lord had overlooked a problem about certain modern-day situations and he had to paraphrase a quote to make it fit."

Debbie sure needed Grandpa and the Bible when she was only sixteen and was thrown out of church.

Until then, she was a very devout churchgoer—and even taught Sunday School. But when she was offered a contract at Warner Bros. to make films and she accepted, the leaders of her church, who considered show business sinful, asked her and her mother to leave the church.

Of course, Debbie went to Grandpa. He must be able to find a quote from the Bible, even if he has to make one up, to help them now. "Whoever travels with the Lord's grace,"

Grandpa told Debbie, "may venture even into Sodom and Gomorah—Ezekiel twelve-fourteen." Debbie says, "I'm sure I saw the wink in his eye."

"If you leave the church," Grandpa said, "it doesn't mean you're leaving God. Maybe this church will leave you, but this God—never."

"What shall I do, Grandpa?" Debbie cried. "Do I study to be a gym teacher or do I go into show business?"

"There's a set of rules in life and living," he answered, "that's been good for hundreds of years, and whoever lives by them has never gone wrong. No matter what your profession or choice of work, you can find these rules in the Bible— Exodus twenty. You learned them in Sunday School as the Ten Commandments. No matter how others behave around you, concentrate on keeping these rules and you will always be able to walk proudly and sleep well—whether you're in show business or digging ditches."

Grandpa's decision has brought joy to millions through the God-given talents of Debbie Reynolds—and after all, that's what God is all about. To paraphrase one of Grandpa's sayings, "Don't judge God's house by any of its members or, come to think of it, by any of its leaders either."

"Since that time," Debbie told me recently, when I visited her backstage when she was starring in *Irene*, "I've faced many problems, big and small, from Eddie Fisher to some I face right now, but in my heart I know the precepts of the Ten Commandments will see me through.

"They have in the past and will in the future."

I had a similar experience when I was a kid starting in show business. I was in love with a reverend's daughter and asked for her hand in marriage. "You're a nice boy, I'm sure," the reverend told me, "but I could never let my daughter marry an actor. I don't want to say they're all bums, but why don't you get another job? An actor—never."

"At least," I pleaded, "why don't you come and see me work? It's an honest profession. Maybe you'll like me—I'm sure you'll like me. Please come and see my show."

"Okay," he said, "but we could never let our daughter marry an actor."

When I saw the old man in the audience that night, I worked harder than I ever did in my life. After the show I ran straight to his house. "Well," I said, "how did you like me?"

"Don't worry, son," he said. "You can marry my daughter —you're not an actor."

Love is Sammy Cahn's business—and don't go thinking evil things. Sammy is one of America's greatest poets. His lyrics to the songs have won him four Academy Awards, including "Three Coins in the Fountain," "All the Way," "High Hopes," and "Call Me Irresponsible"—as well as the only "Emmy" ever awarded for a song, namely "Love and Marriage."

Sammy's home was always filled with love and love of God —as well as respect for His Commandments. "My father was always governed by the Laws of God," Sammy told me, "and followed them blindly. Naturally, it all rubbed off on me. On the High Holy days, I would go to the synagogue to pay my respect to my father and to God."

On Yom Kippur, the Day of Atonement, they have a special prayer called "Al Chet" which means "for the sin of." It's a form of community confession. Once a year the Jews read all the sins that you can commit, from gossiping to stealing to lying—hundreds of them—and with each sin you read, you bow and bang yourself in the chest—asking forgiveness and hitting yourself for punishment at the same time.

Sammy was watching his father do this for about fifteen minutes. With each "Al Chet" he banged himself harder on the chest. Suddenly, after about thirty or forty "Al Chets," he stopped and said aloud, "What am I hitting myself so hard for? I haven't done anything."

It's love and prayer that put Sammy on the road to God. This modern-day Byron was brought up in a religious home and was prepared for his bar mitzvah ritual. "I must say," Sammy told me modestly, "that I brought it off with the required skill so that I didn't embarrass my mother, who leaned on me to do it—or my father, who just glowed through it. It

201

was during this religious training by the rabbi, who came to the house, because I somehow could never find the route to his little synagogue, that I picked up a little bit of Hebrew prayer that has served me ever since.

"In case of a tie—this is the little prayer I say before I close my eyes. It is in Hebrew so I will try to say the words phonetically and translate:

UH-NUH AHDENOY	I ask you dear God
HUH-SHEE-UH-NOY	To help me God
UH-NUH-AHDENOY	I ask you dear God
HAH-TZLICH-UH NOY	To bless me God

"Having said this in the Hebrew, I address myself to God in English and say, 'Dear God, please help me to be a good husband (I have a wife). Make me a good father (I have a daughter Laurie and a son Steve). Make me a good brother, (I have four sisters—Sadye, Pearl, Florence and Evelyn—I am an only son). Make me a good friend (I am a fortunate man because I have many many friends and want to be deserving of their friendship). Make me a good citizen, (I am an American and believe it is a blessing many, too many, take too lightly, and I pray to be deserving of this blessing). Finally I say, above all make me a decent human being, because I am aware that this is the great, great miracle of all. Finally, I say Amen and go to sleep!

"Now, this seems like a long drawn out prayer but if you eliminate the parenthetical commentary it goes rather quickly and doesn't take more than a moment to say. It is not only important that I am communicating with God, but that I am bringing to mind my blessings in the form of the people I love and the things I love, and love is important and love, I think, is God! If that theory is even close to true then I work with God all the time, because the word "love" is the main commodity in my work, which is lyrics. Now, if you will accept that God is Love or Love is God, then I ask you to accept that His cathedral and/or synagogue is the heart. So then, I come to a lyric (rather sneakily I guess) written for the TV special, "Our Town," based on the play by the extremely gifted Thornton Wilder. This TV special played only one time and was never seen again. In it Frank Sinatra sang these words to the beautiful music of James Van Heusen:

Look to your heart
When there are words to say
And never leave your love unspoken

Day by day
We go our thoughtless way
And only when we pray
Do we remember those we love

Too late we find
A word that's warm and kind
Is more than just a passing token

Speak your love
To those who seek your love
Look to your heart
Your heart will know what to say
Look to your heart today!!!

Bob Hope has been on the "Road to God," ever since he got his first laugh.

"Thou wilt shew me the path of life: In thy presence is fullness of joy; at they right hand there are pleasures for evermore." (Psalms 16:11)

"The most important thing laughter can do," Bob told me, "is to bring back the will to live—and, when the time comes, to give us courage to go with good cheer.

"I've seen the ones who aren't going to make it—boys smiling their way right up to St. Peter's gate, and I've got a hunch they're holding a sure pass. Like one young soldier I saw in Vietnam. He was stretched out on the ground getting a blood transfusion. 'I see they're giving you the old raspberry, son,' I said.

" 'It sure feels good,' he laughed. 'The guy who gave this must have been tax exempt or raised his own beef. It's strong stuff.'

" 'Before I had gotten twenty yards,' Bob said, 'he had gone his way, smiling.' "

Hope told me that when he visits those service hospitals anyplace around the world, they expect him to "louse up the joint." Otherwise, it wouldn't be Bob Hope. It's what they look forward to—and Bob never disappoints them.

"One thing they don't want is sympathy," Bob says. "They want me to walk into a ward filled with guys harnessed to torturous contraptions and say, 'Don't get up, fellows.'

"When I come to a Christmas party, if I notice the lone star atop the pathetic Christmas tree, I'm supposed to say, 'Don't tell me a brigadier general is running this show too.'

"So I say it. And when people wonder how a guy can go on and on like that—well, the answer is that the results themselves keep you up. You can't possibly not do it. The power works both ways. You are sustained by their laughter."

I remember going into St. Alban's Hospital with a troupe of minstrels to cheer up the boys who had just come back from Vietnam. We were there even before their families could see them. Most of them couldn't leave their beds or their chairs.

As we approached one of the wards, I heard someone singing above the clatter of our entrance. Then I noticed the crooner. He was pushing himself towards us in a wheelchair. By the power of his two arms—the only useful limbs he had left.

"Say," I greeted him, "we're supposed to entertain you—and here you are meeting us with a song."

His answer will sustain me always. He said, "When I stopped looking at what I had lost, and began looking at all I had left, I could sing again."

"If you do a good job for others," Bob Hope told me, "you heal yourself at the same time. Laughter can transcend all barriers—even beyond reason, prejudice and cynicism.

"In a jungle I heard the jokes of padres lift GIs' spirits into wanting the fearlessness and gaiety of the men of God, when

204

no amount of solemn approach would have inspired them."

Bob told me he once heard a minister devastate a profane comedian with quiet wit.

It happened at an officers' club. After a pointless and slightly blasphemous story, the alleged comic noticed all eyes were suddenly fastened on the collar insignia of a pleasant, quiet man at the end of the table.

"F'r crissake," blustered the story-teller, "are you a chaplain?"

With a light smile and deliberate emphasis, the chaplain answered, "Yes, for Christ's sake, I am."

Comedian Joe E. Brown used to say, "Laughter is a sharing pleasure."

When he lost his son in World War II, he mentally adopted all the men in the service as his sons. He gave hundreds of shows around the world to bring laughter to the man on the battle fronts.

"Laughter," Joe E. told me, "is healing, and laughter is holy. I could not be interested in any man's religion if his knowledge of God didn't bring him more joy, did not brighten his life, and did not make him want to carry this light into every dark corner of the world. I have no understanding of a long-faced Christian. If God is anything, He must be joy."

When you are laughing, you are sharing of the joy of God.

I don't want to imply that Isaiah or John were stand-up comics or comedy writers, but you'll have to admit that their one-liners will last longer than those of Henny Youngman, Milton Berle or even Bob Hope.

"These things have I spoken unto you, that my joy might remain in you, and that your joy might be full." (John 15:11)

The prophet Isaiah pronounced that the Spirit of the Lord God was upon him not only to comfort all that mourn but to give them "the oil of joy." (Isaiah 61:1–3)

Every time I met my old beautiful friend Maurice Chevalier, he seemed gay and alive and happy. "How do you always manage to be so cheerful?" I asked him one time.

"Of course," he replied, "I don't always feel gay. If I did I would be what you call 'slap-happy.' But the moment I feel an audience responding to the gaiety I am trying to give out, I feel gaiety coming back to me. It's like a boomerang—a blessed boomerang.

This is true not only for the entertainer. It's a game anybody can play.

"You go to your office. You're grouchy—you growl a good-morning to your secretary. She may have been in a good mood until then, but immediately the ugliness is contagious, and she is now grouchy to the next person she talks to. In reverse, you come in whistling or singing. You extend a happy greeting. It boomerangs—the girl brightens and so does the entire office."

It's true. There are targets everywhere. Just take aim and shoot from the lip—with joy. Hate begets hate and joy begets joy.

I saw a sign on a New York City bus that tells the story pretty well:

"Doctors tell us that hating people can cause ulcers, heart attacks, headaches, skin rashes and asthma—it doesn't make the people you hate feel too good either."

Nobody can live in a world by himself. Anything you do to help others helps you. Anything you do to hurt others hurts you. If you deceive others, you deceive yourself.

This is the truth that will simplify your life. It's the truth that will set you free.

The Bible says: "Love one another . . . that is My commandment." That's why it's so much better to send out a little love. It's bound to become a "blessed boomerang."

What is love? How do you recognize it? What does it look like? St. Augustine had the answer:

Love has the hands to help others.
It has the feet to hasten to the poor and needy.
It has eyes to see misery and want.
It has the ears to hear the sighs and
    sorrows of men.
That is what love looks like.

Van Johnson has always had the capacity to love and laugh at others as well as himself. It's how he overcame two cancer operations and a couple of major automobile accidents.

In spite of all the heartaches that he has endured, I never met Van that he wasn't filled with the "oil of joy."

As he was lying in the hospital after the accident, he talked to God personally. "I'm not ready to go yet, God. Look at my palm—I have a long life line." We know God must have the greatest sense of humor—and Van is around to prove it—looking and feeling better than ever.

"It's prayer," the movie star told me, "pure and simple. I go to all churches. Synagogues as well as Catholic and Protestant houses of worship. Why not? They're all God's houses. When a lot of doctors gave me up, God didn't—and neither did the people of all the nationalities who prayed for me. I felt their prayers—Jew as well as Christian.

"I've had a wonderful life," Van told me. "When they told me I had the 'big C,' I asked myself, is that how it ends? And then I got a call from Roz Russell. When I told her, she went to work immediately. 'We'll get you the best doctors,' she said. 'Of course, the greatest healer is God. Contemplate God. I don't believe your show is over. You're just not ready for the finale. God is still writing the script.'

"I believed her—like I believe God. I trust Him. I was never afraid. It's what kept my show going for a long run."

I bumped into Van recently and he was joyous as always. Just as he was when he was in the chorus at the Roxy Theatre, or playing straight on the borscht belt, or starring on stage or screen. "How are you, pal Joey?" he asked gleefully, as he embraced me.

"Okay, I guess." I answered.

"Okay?" he screamed, "okay? You should be marvelous. You're God's perfect child. He put you here to glorify Him. Let's see some of that glory."

"It's been a tough day," I answered solemnly, "I—"

"A tough day?" he shouted. "This is the day the Lord has made—rejoice—be good—give thanks," he quoted from a beautiful hymn.

I felt better already. "You're so right," I said. "But with the world in chaos, it's pretty tough to throw around glory or joy."

"Joy is not out there," Van reminded me. It's within you. The Kingdom of God is in *you*. Only you can give it to the world. Let me tell you a wonderful story:

This man was so disgusted with the anarchy going on everywhere, that when he came across a picture of the world in a magazine, he tore it to little pieces. His youngest son picked up all the pieces and put them together again.

"How did you put it together so fast?" his father asked.

"I didn't put the world together," the youngster replied. "There was a picture of Christ on the other side—I put *that* together."

Chapter 18.

The Astronauts

The first thing our astronauts did when they reached the moon was pray—from there it was only a local call.

You would pray too if you realized that everything that makes that spacecraft go was supplied by the lowest bidder.

It happens that I'm a big fan of the astronauts. I was thrilled to see them take a walk in space—I've wanted to do the same thing many times when they start to show some of those movies on the plane.

On Christmas Eve of 1968 as astronauts Frank Borman, William Anders and James Lovell were circling the moon and talking to over a billion people on television and radio all over the world, they suddenly introduced a bit that floored everybody from Cape Kennedy to downtown Leningrad.

They began reading, with great reverence, the Biblical account of the creation: "In the beginning, God created the heaven and the earth. . . ."

The reaction to this humble testimony of faith was to millions the most inspiring and moving moment of Apollo 8's dramatic flight. Isn't it interesting that men who rely on the most modern instruments of science should at that moment

211

have the need to read the ancient words of the Bible.

And so the Genesis creation story became part of man's first flight to the moon. Of course, there were some of the usual crank letters demanding that we prohibit astronauts from expressing their views in this way.

But most of the hundred thousand letters or more loved them for it. One prisoner wrote, "In five minutes the astronauts had done more to organize love than all the pickets had done in a hundred years." A bishop from Guatemala said, "The astronauts had done more to catch the ear of the young people than a dozen committees had done in five years."

The Jews expressed their thanks that they had chosen a selection from the Old Testament. The Catholics were thrilled that prayer had become fashionable again. But the letters that meant the most to all the astronauts were those that came from behind the Iron Curtains—from Romania, Bulgaria, Poland, East Germany, Russia, Czechoslovakia and points east—all embracing them for their story of faith.

Colonel Frank Borman said later: "The reading from Genesis from the moon is history now. I would like the record to show the excitement we felt as we rounded the dark side of the moon and saw the Earth appear to rise up out of darkness.

"To me the timing was perfect. . . . A few minutes later we read the creation story. Perhaps, indeed, the Earth is just coming out of darkness into a new kind of creation."

Which reminds me of the story they are telling in Poland. While Gherman Titov, the Russian astronaut was orbiting the earth he suddenly felt a tap on his shoulder. It was God, who asked what he'd seen. Titov said he'd flown over the United States, saw the people frightened and saw them arming. He'd flown over Russia, where he also saw frightened people and a nation arming. But, said Titov, in Poland the people weren't frightened, nor were they arming.

"You mean," God asked, "in Poland they're still depending on Me?"

When "The Unsinkable Molly Brown," with astronauts Grissom and Young, began its first orbit, Young said, "Gahdam-

212

mit—look at that view." He repeated the expletive, "Gahdam-mit. . . ." Grissom, who'd been up there before, cautioned his colleague: "John, they're tape-recording everything we say—and besides, up here we're very close to Him. . . ."

Astronaut Neil Armstrong was a flying bug from the time he was two years old and his parents took him to the Cleveland Airport to see his first plane.

He worked after school to get enough money to pay for his flying lessons and by the time he was fifteen he was a pretty good flier. It's just about then that his career almost ended, too.

A friend of his had an airplane accident and died in his arms. His parents thought now he would stop flying. He was disconsolate for days. He saw no one and talked to no one. Then he came across an old Sunday school notebook in his room. He inadvertently turned to one of the pages which he had written in his own childish hand: "The character of Jesus," and had listed ten qualities of His. "He was sinless, He was humble, He championed the poor, He was unselfish." But the one that hit him where he needed it was number eight—"He was close to God."

And that's when he decided to go on flying.

"I asked God for strength and the right words—and He gave them to me," Neil Armstrong said.

An astronaut is the only man who can see the shape of the world as it really is. That's why every one of them goes to God when they are up there.

Buzz Aldrin worked harder preparing his communion service for the first lunar landing, than he did with the sophisticated tools of the space effort. He knew that it was possible for science to let him down, but God—never.

On the day of the moon landing, Neil Armstrong, Mike Collins and Aldrin awoke at 5:30 A.M. Neil and Buzz separated from Mike in the command module. Their powered descent was right on schedule, except Neil had to steer the spacecraft, *Eagle,* to a better terrain. With only seconds worth of fuel left, they finally touched down at 3:30 P.M.

213

Now Neil and Buzz were sitting inside the *Eagle,* while Mike circled in lunar orbit, unseen in the black sky above them. This was the moment for communion.

Aldrin called back to Houston. "Houston, this is *Eagle.* This is the LM pilot speaking. I would like to request a few moments of silence. I would like to invite each person listening in, wherever and whomever they may be, to contemplate for a moment the events of the past few hours and to give thanks in his own individual way."

For Buzz Aldrin and the other astronauts, this meant taking communion. In the radio blackout he opened the little plastic packages which contained bread and wine and poured the wine into the chalice his church had given him. "It was exciting to think," Buzz said, "that the very first liquid ever poured on the moon and the first food eaten there, were communion elements.

"And so, just before I partook of the elements, I read the words which I had chosen to indicate our trust that as man probes into space we are in fact acting in Christ."

He read, "I am the vine—You are the branches. Whoever remains in Me, and I in him, will bear much fruit; for you can do nothing without Me." (John 15:5)

The astronauts proved to us that the entire space program is worth it, if it can bring us all together again—especially in our belief and trust in the Lord. Then it doesn't matter what it costs us. And if you think the space program is expensive now, wait till they make the astronauts join a union and they start charging by the mile.

As America's first man in orbit, Colonel John H. Glenn, Jr., of New Concord, Ohio, became one of the greatest public heroes in history. Already famed as a marine test pilot, combat flier in World War II and the Korean War, recipient of five distinguished flying crosses, Colonel Glenn flew into immortality and the admiration of the entire free world, when on February 20, 1962, he piloted the space capsule *Friendship 7* three times around the globe. With this one brave blast off into the sunlit void, astronaut Glenn provided a couple of hundred million Americans with their sharpest thrill and strongest moral tonic since our Union began.

"When I was selected for the U.S. Space Program," Colonel Glenn says, "one of the first things given me was a space handbook put out by the government. It contains one paragraph about the hugeness of the universe which impressed me very much: 'When we recall that our galaxy is some 100,000 light years in diameter, the sun being an insignificant star some 30,000 light years from the galactic center, circling in an orbit of its own every 200 million years as the galaxy rotates, we realize that even trying to visualize the tremendous scale of the universe beyond the solar system is difficult, let alone trying to attempt physical exploration and communications. Nor is the interstellar space of the galaxy the end, for beyond are the millions of other galaxies, all apparently rushing from one another at fantastic speeds. The limits of the telescopically observable universe extend at least two billion light years from us in all directions.' "

I don't even understand the question. But Glenn is making a point.

"Now, what is the point I'm making? It is the orderliness of the whole universe about us, from the smallest atomic structure to the greatest thing we can visualize: galaxies, millions of light years across, all traveling in exact prescribed orbits in relation to one another.

"Could this all have just happened? Was it an accident that someone tossed up a bunch of flotsam and jetsam which suddenly started making these orbits all of its own accord? I can't believe that is really true. I think it was a definite plan. This is one big thing in space that shows me there is a God, some power that put all this into orbit and keeps it there. It wasn't just an accident."

Colonel John Glenn, Jr., has shown us the way in space and in God. "Jesus had His beliefs," says Glenn, "and He had the courage of his convictions to act upon them, to live by them.

He believed. He acted. These guidelines guided Christ in His everyday life when He was here on Earth. The guidelines He used are available to us today, and they are just as timeless as they were in Jesus' time.

"These guidelines apply just as much to one business as they do to another. But the choice is ours. We are the ones who have to make the choice. God hasn't said, 'You *will* do this.' We have been placed here as free agents to decide whether we will or will not live by these guidelines. The choice is ours."

The astronauts and the moon flights brought more joy and consequently more jokes than any events in history:

In China, the space program was hit with a terrible blow when with only minutes before takeoff, the astronauts ate the fortune cookies that held the flight plan.

You think you got trouble? I know one astronaut who got on a scale and his fortune read: "Beware of long trips."

When one astronaut was asked to lecture to a class of future space men, his big advice was: "The whole secret is—don't look down!"

When the astronauts found out they were allowed 110 pounds of recreational equipment, one of them requested Raquel Welch.

All the astronauts brought joy, confidence, hope and courage, as well as faith to a troubled world. One astronaut whose faith will always live is Edward H. White II.

When Astronaut White took *Gemini IV* flight into history, he took along a St. Christopher medal, a gold cross and a star of David. "I took these things," he said later, "to express the great faith I had in the people and the equipment we were using for the mission. I had faith in myself, and in Jim McDivitt who was my partner, and especially in my God. Faith was the most important thing I had going for me on the flight. I couldn't take something for every religion in the country, but I took the three with which I was most familiar."

216

The response to this story was phenomenal—especially from young people who seemed surprised that an astronaut could be interested in religion—and in all religions.

As a final meaning of this gesture, astronaut White wrapped up the three symbols—the St. Christopher medal, the cross and the star of David in two small flags: "An American one, indicating that in our country we live in brotherhood under one flag, differing yet united, and a United Nations flag, representing my hope that someday all the world will live in brotherhood."

A few times during the trip there could have been some serious incidents because of some malfunction of equipment but "It was the faith we had in our training, in each other, and in our God that didn't leave room for negative thoughts. I carried the three symbols with me at all times."

When the youngsters later asked questions about what they stood for, it gave Colonel White a chance to tell them that "Man was being drawn closer together as never before. The space program is progressively decreasing the size of the world. Eventually, if we are to survive, people will just have to get along better and settle their differences like good neighbors.

"When I wrapped the cross and the St. Christopher medal and the Star of David in those little flags, I was saying, in an action, a prayer that is on so many of our lips today; the seeking prayer that pleads for a true brotherhood for all mankind."

Here is Colonel Edward H. White's favorite prayer, from the West Point Cadet's Prayer:

Oh God, our Father, Thou searcher of men's hearts, Help us to draw nearer to Thee in sincerity and truth. . . . Make us to choose the harder right instead of the easier wrong, and never to be content with a half truth when the whole can be won.

Endow us with courage that is born of loyalty to all that is noble and worthy, that scorns to compromise with vice

217

and injustice, and knows no fear when truth and right are in jeopardy. . . .

Kindle our hearts in fellowship with those of a cheerful countenance and soften our hearts with sympathy for those who sorrow and suffer. . . .

Help us, in our work and in our play, to keep ourselves physically strong, mentally awake and morally straight, that we may better maintain the honor of the Corps untarnished . . . to realize the ideals of West Point in doing our duty to Thee and to our country.

Chapter 19.

———⊶⊷———

There Are Vitamins in a
Word of Praise

I once had a nightmare. I dreamed I was working to a packed theatre and nobody laughed, cheered or applauded. Even at fifty thousand a week that would be murder. So you can imagine how I felt at my salary.

Everybody could use a word of praise—especially the famous. In the world of the superstar the knife is always out. Often the blade is unsheathed thoughtlessly. The civilians who comprise the great unwashed, figure that wrapped up in your money and fame, you're completely insulated. They figure you don't really hear it when they see you on the street and stop you and say, "Hey, you're much older looking in person, you know that?" or "How come you're so much fatter off the screen?"

Milton Berle developed a stock answer when a square approached him with, "How come you look younger on camera?" Yawned Milton time after time, "You've got an old set."

Maybe they think that celebrities don't have any feelings. Maybe they think show people aren't human. Maybe they think these conscious or unconscious insults don't penetrate us. The truth is, in some cases they are never forgotten.

221

Carol Burnett says, "Let's face it. I have attracted the type who drags a homely kid with huge buck teeth up to me saying, 'See, my daughter looks just like you. Talk to her. Make her feel good. She thinks she's ugly because she looks like you.'

"Once," continued Carol, "a guy stopped dead on Broadway, pointed wildly and hollered, 'Hey, aren't you what's-er-name? God, if it ain't you-know-who!' So thrilled was he that he grabbed a stranglehold and carted me back to where his wife stood, screaming, 'Look, it's whodoyoucallit. She ain't such a dog!'

"One advantage of being a comic," explains Carol, "is you can turn these hideous, embarrassing situations into funny ones, cover up those searing insecurities. Otherwise, these incidents can shorten your life."

I shall never forget the recent attempt on my life. It so happens that I looked beautiful that particular day. I had on a white suit, a tan, a brand-new haircut and manicure and was admiring myself in the mirror before I showed myself to the outside world.

"How many great men are there in the world?" I asked Cindy as I primped in the mirror.

"One less than you think," she said.

I knew she was kidding because it was my day. I never looked better in my life. I strutted out of my apartment and into my white Rolls and sailed down Fifth Avenue. I stopped for gas and got out of my car to let my full glory blind anyone within eyeshot of the pump.

One elderly man tapped me on the shoulder and said, "Excuse me, Mr. Adams, my mother would like to see you. She's in the car over there." I figured it must be an elderly lady if she was his mother, so I would go to her—and anyway, I really looked great and could use a word of praise.

The lady in back of the beat up Ford looked like she was 130 years old. She took up the entire back seat of the car—weighed at least four hundred pounds. She had no teeth, her hair was all over her face and she was wearing what looked like an unmade bed. "Joey Adams," she greeted me. "How did you let yourself get like that?"

And that was my best day. I slumped back into my Rolls and drove home. I didn't show my face and body for the rest of the week. I stayed home and reread all my scrapbooks ten times before I could go out in the open again.

It's not only the performer who needs the encouragement. Without praise or sign of appreciation, all of us can lose self-confidence or desire.

My niece was telling me about her daughter who sometimes misbehaves and has to be put down. But one day she had been a particularly good kid. She hadn't done one single thing that needed scolding. "That night, after I tucked her in bed," my niece told me, "I heard my daughter sobbing. When I turned back, I found her head buried in her pillow. Between sobs she asked, 'Haven't I been a *fairly* good girl today?'"

It is more important to recognize a good deed than it is a bad one. My nephew once complained, "What's the use of doing good? Daddy never notices it."

There are vitamins in a word of praise. Kindness is one thing you can't give away—it comes back to you.

Be kind to your mother-in-law—babysitters are expensive.

And be kind to the lady you're married to—the wife you save may be your own.

Many a marriage has been saved by the right word at the right time. Women have a pretty good knack for such things.

I know a couple that were married on February 13. "I could only tell you," he told his wife, "that I will never forget our wedding anniversary. It will always be the day after Lincoln's birthday." His wife answered, "And I will never forget Lincoln's birthday—it will always be the day before we were married."

You always remember a kind deed—especially if it was yours. The trick is to know how to take a word of praise as well as give it.

Bob Hope said to Julie London, "I've known you for years

—and you haven't changed an inch." It was just what Julie needed at that moment to make her feel like a queen.

Betty Grable seemed to be down and thinking her age when she joined me in Baltimore to start rehearsing for *Guys and Dolls,* in which we were co-starring. "Say," I greeted her, "the years have touched you with a feather." Her shoulders pulled back, the smile spread all over her face, and once again she looked like the pinup girl of World War II.

A word of praise costs nothing—but it gives so much riches. If you won't take it from me, take it from Proverbs 3:27: "Withhold not good from them to whom it is due, when it is in the power of thine hand to do it."

Jimmy Stewart has received every kind of accolade as a motion picture star—but the greatest words of love he ever received came from his dad and actually saved his life.

During World War II Jimmy enlisted in the Air Corps and became part of a bomber squadron. "Alone in my bunk one night," Colonel Stewart recalls, "I opened a letter which read, 'My dear Jim, I know you are in danger every minute, but I am banking on the enclosed copy of the 91st Psalm. The thing that takes the place of fear and worry is the promise in these words. I am staking my faith in these words. I feel sure that God will lead you through this mad experience . . . I can say no more. I only continue to pray. God bless you and keep you. I love you more than I can tell you. Dad.'

"Never before had he said he loved me. I always knew he did, but he had never said it until now. I wept. In the envelope there was a small booklet bearing the title *The Secret Place— A Key to the 91st Psalm.* I began to read it. From that day, the little booklet was always with me.

"Before every bombing raid over Europe, I read some of it, with each reading the meaning deepened for me:
'I will say of the Lord, he is my refuge and my fortress . . . His truth shall be thy shield and buckler. Thou shalt not be afraid for the terror by night; nor for the arrow that flieth by day. . . . For He shall give His angels charge over thee, to keep thee in all thy ways. They shall bear thee up in their hands, lest thou dash thy foot against a stone.'

224

"And I was borne up. Dad had committed me to God, but I felt the presence of both throughout the war."

Praise is love and love is praise. It can move mountains as well as hearts. Something good can be said about everyone. We have only to say it.

A schoolteacher I know tells the story of a young lad of thirteen who came into her class sloppy, sickly looking, speaking badly, and sad. Sympathy overpowered her and she decided to do all she could to give him a sense of belonging. But how?

"Since man is created in God's image," she reasoned, "there must be something good in each individual. Looking at Tommy, I had to search for something to praise. He was bad in reading, horrible in arithmetic and not good in spelling. Also, he didn't get on too well with the other children.

"Then, one day, I discovered that he had quite a pleasing and sweet voice. I immediately complimented him on it and the effect was miraculous. His manner improved. He started combing his hair. He became one of the group.

"For our Christmas program, Tommy was chosen to sing the only solo. Some weeks later when the school principal visited our class, he stopped in front of Tommy's desk. Tommy was embarrassed; he realized he should have been working in a much higher grade. Suddenly he looked up and announced with pride, 'I'm teacher's *best* singer.'

"In the years since," this loving teacher says, "I have had other 'Tommy's in my classes—all with something to praise. But I'll never forget my 'best singer' because he made me realize that every person has at least one talent and the right compliment can help him find it."

One of my great friends is a lawyer whose daughter is an ugly duckling. This has made her arrogant, ungainly and tough to live with. It was almost impossible to find some quality in her to brag about. Sitting around the house at one party he was listening to his friends brag about their children when the unpretty one stumbled in. "My," her father said, "isn't she getting tall." The little girl stopped for a moment, straightened up to her five feet, a smile spread over her face, and she walked away happy as a beauty contest winner.

Everybody, great or obscure is touched by genuine appreciation. George Bernard Shaw heard the young Jascha Heifetz play the violin. He sent him the following note: "Young man—Such perfection annoys the gods. You should play one or two wrong notes after each performance to appease them."

"When Heifetz became Heifetz," says Sam Levenson, the humorist, "I was often compared to him. My family always said to me when I practiced the violin: 'A Heifetz you're *not.*'"

Sam says it was a stranger who gave him the confidence and ambition to go on and become one of the great humorists of our time. The famous Lambs Club had a professional night where the performers got a chance to show their stuff. Levenson was thrilled that he was chosen to appear before his peers in the theatre.

After his spot, the famous show-business historian and humorist Joe Laurie, Jr., sought Sam out and told him, "Hey, kid, from a theatrical point of view, you are doing everything wrong. You're laughing at your own jokes, you got your hand in front of your face when you're talking, you're dressed like a school teacher. *But* don't change a thing—it's what will make you a star."

Everybody needs a word of praise. That's why people look in fortune cookies or your fortune that comes from the penny scale in the drug store. Fulton Oursler tells about Sir Max Beerbohm who went with his aging wife to a theatrical party in London. As they entered the room he was ambushed by a horde of stage and film beauties, all eager to impress the great critic and caricaturist. Beerbohm turned to his wife and said: "Darling, let's find a quiet corner. You are looking so charming tonight that I want to talk to you alone."

One little girl was looking for a word of praise and asked her mom: "How much am I worth to you?"

"A million dollars," Mom answered.

"Can you advance me a quarter?"

Amy Vanderbilt, the author and authority on etiquette says, "We should make better use of our amazing power to appreciate. Anyway it's good etiquette to say thank you—and what better way than with a word of praise.

"I think this is why the Bible tells us so often to give thanks, to praise God, and to acknowledge His benefits. Surely it's not that God, like us, needs appreciation for His own well-being. It must be because He knows that when we learn to give thanks, we are learning to concentrate not on the bad things, but on the good things of our lives."

Giving a gift of appreciation is surely the best example I know to illustrate the Biblical promise: "Give, and it shall be given unto you; good measure, pressed down, and shaken together, and running over." (Luke 6:38)

Let me tell you the story of a poor but ambitious vaudevillian. Show business was his life. When he and his wife found that their act was no more in demand and they were broke, he decided to go to see his friends Al Jolson and Eddie Cantor. "Maybe they'll help me put a new act together," he told his wife, "After all, I did help them when they started."

Jolson was glad to see him. But when the vaudevillian told him he needed five hundred dollars to get himself a new act, Jolson exploded. "Are you kidding? I'll give you a thousand— only get out of this business. You always were a nothing act and you always will be. I tell you what—I'll give you two thousand —open a small candy store—only promise me you'll never set foot on stage again. I love this business too much to see a ham like you spoil it."

The actor walked out before Jolson finished the lecture, without taking the money. When he went to see Eddie Cantor, the comedian couldn't have been nicer. "I always thought you were the greatest act in the business," Eddie said. "I'm sorry I can't spare the money at the moment, it's all tied up in cash, but don't quit. You always had the greatest act in vaudeville and you always will."

"What happened?" his wife asked when he returned to the rooming house. "That phony bum, Jolson," he said. "Imagine offering me two thousand dollars to get out of the business! But that Cantor—now there's a beautiful guy."

You can never measure the good you can do with a word of praise. Anything that makes a child or an adult feel more important about himself is one of the most helpful things that can happen to him. Children who know in their hearts that they themselves are admired or appreciated, find it easy, in turn, to be appreciative of others.

You never know how a kind word helps. One minister received a letter from a very grateful housewife when her husband passed away. "I just had to write and thank you for the beautiful words at Charlie's funeral. You said such wonderful things about him, for a minute I wasn't sure you were talking about my Charlie."

Everybody has a craving to be appreciated and a word of praise brings out the best in us. What does it cost to tell the cabdriver that it was a pleasant ride? He's bound to be nicer to his next passenger. Especially if you didn't forget to tip him. How much could it hurt you to say to your customer, "Have a nice day," or "Thank you—come again."

Send a note of thanks to a performer you liked—or the author of a good story in the paper or a program you enjoyed on the air.

Billy Graham says, "Send you wife some flowers once in a while, even without a reason, and just say I love you. She may fall down at first, but you'll notice that she'll dress up for you when you come home—and the dinners will be better and so will the kisses."

It's not necessary to always be too truthful when it comes to critical opinions. When I go to a show and I must go backstage to see the actors, I can always find something nice to say without hurting them even when the show is bad. I remember seeing my good friend Milton Berle in some show that really bombed. This was a tough one. But when I went backstage after the performance, I simply said, "Well, Milton, you did it again." This satisfied him, and took me off the hook.

Ed Sullivan's beloved wife Sylvia watched every one of his Sunday night TV shows at home and he rushed to call her after the program to find out the real opinion. Even on bad nights she had something good to say, or at least it sounded good. "There was something there for everybody," or "It was sure different," or "Ed, you looked great," or "That was really a show." Ed was satisfied and everybody was happy.

I remember Earl Wilson's review of a bad nightclub show. Earl didn't want to hurt the cast or the producer, but he just couldn't rave this one, so he said, "The food was great, the room was perfectly air-conditioned, the waiters wore beautiful red jackets and the sound and lighting were just perfect. Tomorrow night I will review the Copa show."

"If the need for appreciation is so universal," Amy Vanderbilt asks, "Why is it most of us are stingy with our words of thanks?"

There are so many stories in the Bible that bring this out. One of the most poignant is Luke's account of the day that Jesus healed ten lepers, and only one returned with a word of thanks.

"Were not all ten cured?" asked Jesus. "Where are the other nine?"

Even critics could use a nice word once in a while. Rex Reed is a gentle man who happens to be a critic. "I firmly believe we are here for a purpose." he says. "I don't think we arrived here accidentally—otherwise we would not be as intelligent as we are. If I thought otherwise, I would have no desire to criticize or give my opinions or have any desire to continue my life with its pain and its disillusionment. It must be leading somewhere that's more important than what's going on here. Yes, I do believe there is a life after death."

You can imagine that a nice, gentle man like that could

never hurt anybody intentionally. It pains him to write a bad review. One time he was forced to write a tough criticism of a Steve Lawrence album. He really was sad about it until Steve called and said: "Say, Rex, you were right. You helped me a lot with that review. Edie and I agree with you. Thanks for telling me." Rex needed a kind word at that moment more than Steve or Edie—and it came from the source that could help him.

Renowned author Isaac Asimov joined a new publishing firm and handed in his manuscript. Some time later he received a letter from one of the editors telling him that he would have to make certain changes before his book could be accepted. When the senior editor heard about the letter he was furious at this young editor for sending that kind of note to such an important author. Of course, the young man was now worried about his job until Asimov arrived at the office one day and told the young editor in front of his boss, "You are right. Thanks for the help. I should have thought of those things myself. I promise I'll make those changes as soon as possible." That young editor became Isaac's fan for life.

What good is wearing a new tie if nobody notices it? Why bother to get all dressed up if nobody compliments you?

The great Florenz Ziegfeld used to spend two or three hundred dollars for undergarments for his showgirls that nobody ever saw. I once asked him about that. "Why should you spend so much money for underwear for your girls that nobody knows they are wearing?"

"But," he answered, "the girls know."

One of my good friends is Oscar Rose, the announcer on my WEVD radio show. I like him because he always has a kind word to say to put you in a better mood. His usual greeting is, "I feel better now," and if you ask, "I didn't know you were ill," he answers, "No, I feel better—now that I've seen you."

Morey Amsterdam really goes to extremes. He likes everybody. He can find something good in everybody and every-

230

thing. "This steak is the greatest. . . . Doesn't she sing great? . . . Did you ever see such a clean shirt? . . . Doesn't she have nice ankles?"

One day I did get a little annoyed at him. "Okay," I said, "you think everybody is great—Now, tell me one nice thing you can find about Adolph Hitler?"

"Well," he answered, "I admit I don't get choked up when I hear his name, but you must admit he was the best in his line."

I was particularly grateful to Pearl Bailey for doing a benefit for the Actors Youth Fund and called her to say thanks. "God bless you," I said. "He always has," she answered.

Walter Winchell was the hottest reporter on the air. His Sunday night broadcast was heard by "Mr. and Mrs. America and all the ships at sea." On one train trip an elderly lady sat down next to the columnist and said, "Mr. Winchell, in our house we never miss your broadcasts. We believe you—and we trust you—don't ever lie to us."

Walter told me that every time he did a broadcast after that, he saw the face of this little old lady in the microphone. "She was watching over me to make sure I tell the truth, the whole truth and nothing but the truth."

When the beloved comedian Ed Wynn died, the family really needed a word of love. At the funeral somebody said, "That's the first time Ed Wynn made us cry." He will never know what those words meant to his loved ones.

When Eddie Cantor went to his dressing room in heaven, somebody remarked, "When he died, even the undertaker was sorry."

Ed Sullivan is one of the nicest men in the history of show business—and the most thoughtful. He is always there with a kind word. I appeared on so many of his Sunday night shows with almost every kind of act in the business—from the singing dentists to the Fire Island fife and drum corps. On one of his

231

last shows he put me in a dressing room with the monkey act. I was a little embarrassed—and besides the monkey didn't smell too good.

About five minutes before the show, Ed walked into the dressing room to say his usual kind word. "I'm sorry we had to put you two together," he said. "Oh, I answered politely, "that's okay—I understand."

"I wasn't talking to you," he answered.

I was a great friend of the late and great Lyndon Baines Johnson, the thirty-sixth president of the United States. This friendship took a terrible beating one morning a few years ago. Let me tell you the story.

I became an actor because I like to sleep late. So, whenever we get a new housekeeper my wife warns her that I am not to be awakened for any reason or anyone. Whenever I get up, no matter what time it is, that's when she gives me my messages.

"They can say it's the mayor, the governor, or even the President of the United States. Nobody wakes Mr. Adams until he gets up himself."

I learned a long time ago that anything can wait a couple of hours—and the guy that says he's the head of MGM and it's a matter of life and death, usually wants you for a benefit anyway.

President Lyndon Johnson was a telephone caller. He often made his own calls—dialed himself—especially when he wanted a fast answer.

He called me one morning before twelve. My new Estonian housekeeper answered. "I'd like to talk to Joey Adams, please," the man said.

"He's sleepin'," said Marta.

Of course, she could have said I'm in conference or I'm out —or I'm busy. Anything. But at 11:30 you just don't tell the President, "He's sleepin'."

"But," said the man on the phone, "this is the White House."

"Look, buster," Marta answered haughtily, "I don't care what color is your house. He don't talk to nobody till he gets up."

"But this is the President. . . ."

"I don't care if it's the President of the United States of America," she bellowed.

"But this *is* the President. . . ."

"So call back!" and she hung up.

When I awoke at the crack of one, I asked for my messages. Marta was not too good at writing messages. Only an Estonian pharmacist could read them. Also, she was running the vacuum cleaner when I asked and it wasn't important enough to stop and talk to me. So, from memory, which wasn't too good, she reeled off the messages.

"Your wife from NBC called," like I have a wife at every network. "Oh, yes, and some man with a low voice said you should meet him I forgot where. And an agent with a long name said you should call him. I forgot when."

"Anything else?" I asked.

"Oh, yes," she mumbled. "Some angry president from a white house called."

That's how I discovered the President of the United States wanted to see me to present me with the LBJ medal. It was only days before he decided he was not going to run again.

LBJ was so depressed when I visited the White House that sad day. Anarchy, violence, revolution and demonstrations were going on all over the country. And he found time to present a medal to just a little guy who likes to tell stories.

My heart went out to him. "Mr. President," I said, "all that hate is organized—and they are the minority. It's about time we organized love—which is the majority. The majority loves you. Please remember that Mr. President."

He kept me there for hours, telling him my favorite stories. It felt so good to hear him laugh out loud. When he walked me to the gate, he put his arm around my shoulders and said, "You're so right. Love is the majority. I'll never forget that. Thank you for reminding me."

There is an old Hebrew legend which says that after God created the world, He called the angels to Him and asked what they thought of it. One of them said, "There is something lacking: the sound of praise to the Creator." So God created music, and it was heard in the whisper of the wind, and in the song of the birds; and to man also was given the gift of song. And all down the ages this gift of song has indeed proved a blessing to multitudes of souls.

Chapter 20.

Pockets Full of Miracles

"So God created man in His own image, in the image of God created he him; male and female created He them. And God blessed them and said unto them, be fruitful and multiply and replenish the earth and subdue it; and have dominion over the fish of the sea, and over the fowl of the air, and over every living thing that moveth upon the earth . . . and God saw everything that he had made, and, behold, it was very good . . ." (Genesis 1:27, 28, 31)

He made it all—without permission of architects, lawyers, doctors, Mao, Kosygin, Nixon, or even Walter Cronkite.

If He can do all that, don't you think He can help you with your cold—or arthritis—or your marital problems, your love life or your job?

So why don't you go to Him right now? Talk to Him, claim your inheritance. You are His child. Take your rightful place as a true child of God. Tell Him you need a miracle. Demand your share—He's loaded with miracles. He's got pockets full of miracles. He's got rooms full of miracles. They grow on trees if you are in tune with God. All you have to do is pluck them right now—they're yours.

Remember, He gave you dominion over all. Use it. Take over. You have the miracles—they were given to you when you were born. All you need is the secret word "believe." The password is "trust."

And now the biggest miracle of all. I've stopped sermonizing. End of sermon. Beginning of proof.

Ed Sullivan is the greatest promoter of faith, hope and charity: "And now abideth Faith, Hope, Charity, these three; but the greatest of these is Charity." (1 Corinthians 13:13)

Naturally, he was ripe for a miracle or two. "When I recall those early TV years, I also recall a pocketful of miracles," Ed told me recently. "We originated a show in Boston, and later I was to take the cast and do another show for the Marist nuns, who are devoted to the care of lepers.

"In arranging the shows, I had become friendly with the wise and witty Sister Augustine. When we were in Boston for the TV show, we were disheartened by news of a labor strike at CBS. Then came a phone call from Sister Augustine. 'Don't worry, Ed,' she said, 'we will pray for you.'

"That night, during dress rehearsal, all the lights went off all over Boston. We tried to get subsidiary power from an airplane carrier in the harbor. We tried candles and flashlights. We tried everything. Nothing worked. Then the phone rang. It was Sister Augustine again.

" 'We'll pray for you again,' she promised. It was 7:00, an hour before we were to go on the air. At 7:30 the lights went on again all over Boston.

"The millions of people who saw the show that night will never believe my connection. It sure wasn't electrical, but you can bet we were plugged in pretty good—to the Master Electrician of them all."

The Clown Prince in the court of King Sinatra is a great young comedian called Pat Scarnato—baptized in show business as Pat Henry.

Like all good little Italian boys, Pat made his communion and was a devoted member of the Church and a loving son.

238

And like all good little Italian boys, his first thoughts were for his family. As soon as he got his name up in lights, he got his parents a beautiful new home with all the trimmings. "Leave all the old stuff," Pat told them, "I want you to have the best."

His beautiful mom, like all good little Italian mothers, accepted it all reluctantly, more to please her son than herself, but she couldn't leave the rosebush that was in her yard all these years.

The rosebush had been in her back yard since she was married. Her name is Rose, and Pop had given her the rosebush when they were married. She cherished it always. It was a love tree, and it was always in full bloom. Now she couldn't leave it there, so she insisted that Pat have it as a remembrance. "It's my best possession," she said, "and I want you to have it for always."

Of course, Pat put it in his garden. But without Rose's loving care and without her talking to it, the tree soon died. In only weeks, the beautiful rosebush was a sick-looking skeleton. But Pat still kept it there in respect to his mom. He called the tree experts, gardners, agriculturists—but nothing happened. "I guess," Pat told me, "the tree missed Mom too much."

Two years later Rose Scarnato passed on to a world where all the trees were always in bloom. After the funeral, Pat came home and walked out to his garden to talk to his mother's tree —his only contact with her now—and there, on the dead tree, was the most beautiful pink rose—in full bloom, in all its splendor. "A miracle," Pat said, "a true miracle."

Would you believe two miracles in one family? Pat's wife Susan is a love. When the comedian gave her a parrot one Christmas, she immediately made it part of the family. She talked to her, said her prayers with her, and even listened to her gossip.

One day when Susan opened the front door to receive a package, the parrot flew out and away. Poor Susan scoured the neighborhood looking for her friend. She called everybody and anybody to look out for her. She advertised in the papers and on the air—even offered a reward for the safe return of her bird.

After about three months, she received a call from a neighbor who suspected that her parrot was lodged in her pear tree. "As a partridge in a pear tree." Susan rushed to the rescue, only to find that her parrot didn't want to come down. She obviously had been having a great time flying around town with who knows who.

Susan offered her food, she talked to her. It was pretty cold by now and she wanted to take her home and give her the love she needed. But the parrot was ashamed—or frightened—or maybe she wanted one last fling.

Poor Susan went home and prayed with all her might and all her heart. She prayed to St. Francis of Assisi, who is often called the Patron Saint of the Birds, because when he died all the doves hovered over him as if to pay their last respects. Susan prayed all night that her parrot would come home: "Please, St. Francis, you love birds and they love you. We need each other. We love each other. Do something—bring her back to me."

The next morning, the day before Christmas, there was the biggest snowstorm in Long Island's history—a miracle. Susan knew that now her parrot would need her, and the warmth of her home and her love.

She ran the twelve blocks, through the snow, to where her parrot was living now, all the time carrying food in her hand. When she got to the tree, she sang up to her friend and offered her food. The shivering and hungry bird flew down to Susan, who fed her, put her under her coat, took her home—and they lived happily ever after.

Actually, miracles are not miracles to God. They are a way of life with Him. They are everyday happenings if you are tuned in. You never know when or where they will strike—for good.

Bishop Fulton J. Sheen, whose talks are always fashioned with a gentle wit, likes to tell the story of the Irish lady who was traveling between the north and south of Ireland. She had hidden a bottle of liquor in her luggage and when the customs man questioned her about the contents of the bottle, she said, "It's Lourdes water."

When he examined it, he found that it looked and tasted like scotch. "Madam," he said sternly, "this is whiskey."

"Glory be to God," she said, "a miracle."

The miracle in the life of Don Rickles, the insult comedian, is that he has never been attacked. Don swears that in all the years he has been heckling celebrities, as well as civilians, only one person ever really objected to his needling. "I made fun of a ringsider's beard and almost got belted—that dame had no sense of humor."

Don is a very gentle man until he faces an audience—and then he becomes the angry young man. But as soon as the battle is over, he takes his victims to his home for some of his mother's chicken soup, to get them well again.

"I only pick on friends," Don pleads. "After all my insults and immortal putdowns, there is no one I really hate. My style is to rib people I really like. If there was anger in it, it wouldn't be funny."

And he always does it to their faces. To Ernest Borgnine he screamed: "Oh, my God—look at you—anybody else hurt in the accident?"

To Orson Welles: "Who makes your tents?"

To Frank Sinatra: "You've got a great voice—too bad it hasn't reached your throat."

To Jack Benny: "The things he does for his friends can be counted on his little finger."

To Phil Harris: "He taught Dean Martin every drink he knows."

To Bob Hope: "What are you doing here? The government has no troops stationed here."

To Marlon Brando: "I see you're wearing blue jeans and a T-shirt. Thanks for dressing up my show. Did your dump truck break down here."

The biggest stars pay big money to come and sit ringside to be insulted by the Jewish Don. And if he doesn't pick on them they are very unhappy. At one benefit Julius LaRosa asked me if Rickles was angry at him. "Why do you say that?" I asked.

"Well," he said, "he passed me and gave me such a pleasant hello—not even one nasty word. Do you think he's mad? Or maybe ill?"

Don's act is built on one thing: 'If you can't say something nice about the guy, let's hear it.' If he doesn't insult you, it means he doesn't love you.

"If I didn't like them," Don says, "I wouldn't pick on them." Rickles said, "God has the greatest sense of humor. That's why He gave me the confidence to kid people. Laughing at blacks, whites, Poles, Jews, Christians, stars and unknowns alike, helps me to laugh at myself.

Don believes that "confidence is believing in God. After all, that's where I get it all. My mother and dad taught me to believe. I am resentful of implications that comedians can't be religious. I guess they think that as soon as you go into show business you start worshipping idols. As a matter of truth, I am a great student of the Bible and was raised an orthodox Jew. I observe all religious holidays and am very knowledgeable about my faith, but I love to test God's sense of humor. After all, like father, like son, like teacher, like pupil.

"I said during the other show, 'I know exactly what Moses said atop of Mt. Sinai. He said, "This is where we should put the hospital."' I'm sure God is still laughing."

If you look up "miracles" in the dictionary, it means marvel or wonder. It is God's natural marvel. Miracles are "God's wonders to perform."

To God, miracles are natural—so they couldn't be of the supernatural.

Claim your miracle—or your marvel—or your wonder. You are made in the image and likeness of your maker, endowed with all His attributes—Good, Love, Power, Principle, Truth, Joy, Harmony—isn't that the greatest miracle of all?

242

Singing star Vic Damone used the power given to him, to create a miracle that saved a man's life—as well as his own.

Vic said, "I learned the hard way that God is more of a friend to me than I am." When his wife left him, he was ready to give up. When he left the Church because he couldn't receive the Holy Sacraments after the divorce, "I was practically dead—but I just couldn't lie down.

"I went searching all the time—claiming all the attributes I knew I had inherited from God. I found a prayer used in the Bahai religion for moments of difficulty:

> Is there any remover of difficulty save God?
> Say Praise Be to God.
> He is God.
> All are his servants and all abide by His bidding.

"I knew then that I had come to the end of my search," Vic told me. "The Bahai religion was for me."

"Wonderful," I said, "whatever gives you peace. Bishop Fulton Sheen said it perfectly. 'It is not a unity of religion we plead for, but a unity of religious people. We may not be able to meet in the same pew, but we can meet on our knees.'

"That's right," Damone said. "Since God made us to be originals, why stoop to be a copy? When I found my way, I wanted to shout it to the world and share it with everybody. You see, we have no clergy. *We* are the teachers.

"I was on the air with Eddie Hubbard in Chicago talking about my new-found peace. I wasn't trying to convert anybody. I just wanted to share my love.

"I recited my prayer because I wanted to bestow it on all: 'Oh, God, refresh and gladden my spirit. Purify my heart. Illumine my powers. I lay all my affairs in your hands. Thou art my guide and my refuge. I shall no longer be sorrowful and grieved. I will be a happy and joyful being. I shall no longer be full of anxiety. I shall not let trouble harrass me. I shall not dwell on the unpleasant things in life. Oh, God, thou art more a friend to me than I am to myself. I dedicate myself to thee, oh Lord.'"

Just as Vic left the microphone, he received a message to call a number in Chicago. The message said it was an emergency—a matter of life and death.

Still flushed with the glow of his hour of love on the radio show, Vic called the number. The man who answered said: "I just heard you on the air. Do you really believe all that junk? I mean, do you really honestly believe in God?"

"Yes, I do," Vic said. "Look, mister if—"

"I was just going to kill myself. You stopped me. I really have no reason to live. My wife left me, I lost my job, I—do you really believe? What do I have to live for?"

"My wife left me, too," Vic answered calmly. "My career was in bad shape, but when I talked to God, I found that He cared, that He loved me more than anybody, and that *He* was ready to take care of me."

"But," the man cried, "I don't know how to talk to God. What will I say? What would He want with a nobody like me?"

"You don't need special words with God," Vic explained. "He speaks all tongues. He knows your problem before you give it to him. All you have to do is talk to Him. You can bet your life. He'll listen—and help."

"Bet my life? My life wasn't worth anything. Who would care if I got out of this lousy world?"

"God cares," Vic said. "Listen, all Bahai people pray at noon. Try it. Tell all your problems to God every day for the next two weeks. Write this prayer down that I just did on the air, and say it every day for the next two weeks. Talk to Him. Tell Him what you want. Ask for guidance—and if you don't get an answer by then, you still have time to kill yourself. You listened to evil all your life. You certainly can spare God two weeks. What have you got to lose—except your life?"

Vic recited his prayer, "Oh, God, refresh and gladden my spirit . . ." The man wrote it down and hung up.

Vic met the man six months later when he came to see his show. He came backstage with his wife on his arm and the biggest smile on his face. "I did it," he cried, "I did it. I prayed every day like you told me—and it worked. God sure listened. I have my wife back, I have a new job. I realize now we are

244

all born equal. God gives us talent. We must find out what that talent is, and we can get it only through prayer. It works—it works. 'Oh, God, thou art more a friend to me than I am to myself.' "

End of miracle—beginning of life.

The Benediction

Well, the services are over, the sermon is through, and now it's time to pass the hat. Only in addition to putting something in, I hope you were able to get something out of it.

I'm the first to admit that a Billy Graham I'm not. I'm certainly not a Martin Luther King, Jr., or even a Norman Vincent Peale j.g.—but if you were able to get a slice of some goodies that my friends Pearl Bailey or Pat Boone or Sammy or Ethel or Debbie or Alan Young or any of my other pals put in the hat for you, it's better than all the applause I could get.

If any of them reached you with the God Bit, tell them— let them know it. Even more than that, tell God. He's your best pal. He can use some applause, too. Remember, He loves you more than your wife or husband or even your mother—and He's never too busy to say hello.

"How excellent is thy loving-kindness, O God! Therefore, the children of men put their trust under the shadow of thy wings. . . ." (Psalms 36:7)

All the goodies are going stale if nobody uses them. And you don't have to look too far for them. The bluebird of happiness is right there in front of you all the time. Joy is not out there—it's right inside you. Somebody who is a much better writer than I put it this way: "The Kingdom of Heaven is within you."

It reminds me of one of my favorite parables. These days they call them anecdotes:

For years Grandpa Adams was an unhappy, stubborn, cranky, crabby old man. Nobody in the village could please him. Then, without warning, he changed. Overnight he became a gentle, happy optimistic soul. Everybody was amazed. "Grandpa," one villager asked, "what caused you to change all of a sudden?"

"Well," the old gentleman answered, "I've been striving all my life for a contented mind. It's done no good—so I've just decided to be contented without it."

That's it! You have it in your power to collect that peace of mind—the contentment that we all seek. All you have to do is decide to accept it. Only you can do it. I have another parable for you:

The man was crying to the doctor that he was always melancholy, always sad, always unhappy, always going around with a heavy heart. The doctor examined him thoroughly but could find nothing physically wrong with him. He took X-rays, blood tests and allergy tests and came up with nothing.

"There is only one cure for you," the doc said, "Bozo the clown. I've sent dozens of patients to see him and they all came back cured. He can make anybody laugh. He sends waves of joy out to child and grown-up alike. Luckily the circus is in town. So, that's my prescription—go see Bozo the clown."

"But," the man said sadly, *"I am* Bozo the clown."

By all means "Love thy neighbor as thyself," but first love thyself—and enjoy what you have. Will Rogers said it pretty well: "Everybody is ignorant—only on different subjects." We all can't be stars or doctors or lawyers or plumbers—but just remember that they can't do what you can do, either. I'm sure that doctor can't dance as well as you do—or that star can't cook like you can—or that plumber can't be a surgeon—even if he charges more. The lawyer couldn't make bagels or fix fenders or build houses. Whatever you do, do it well, do it better than anybody else, and be proud of it.

And do a lot of praying for it, too. It doesn't mean you'll get everything you want—but it will get you everything you deserve.

Steve Allen says, "Logical common sense indicates that much material prayer is doomed to reap no benefit. When two men, for example, pray for the same thing; when Notre Dame prays to beat Southern Methodist on the football field while Southern Methodist is praying for just the opposite result—it is obvious that Heaven is going to please only one group of supplicants and very probably the one that is better trained.

"The same thing will be true of much prayer that is only entreaty—begging for a handout from Heaven. There are young girls praying for jobs as actresses who could be better off staying home and students praying for help in passing tests for which they have not had the foresight to equip themselves technically. These and millions like them breach religious etiquette, often even asking God to satisfy their desires at the cost of depriving someone else.

"I suppose the most meaningful form of prayer is the prayer of thanksgiving, the prayer for grace, the prayer that we may be given strength to improve our spiritual selves."

What Steve and everybody else have been trying to tell us is that you get what you put into it. William Thackeray said it: "The world is a looking glass and gives back to every man the reflection of his own face." Now, you have to admit that's pretty good.

You can't be a lawyer or a doctor or a scientist without study. You can't play the piano without practice. You can't be a tailor if you don't have a needle and thread. You can't be a plumber without tools. What could Guy Lombardo do with his baton if his band doesn't show up?

It's all up to you. You can have it all if you are willing to put something in the hat yourself. Give God a little help. "Even faith as of a grain of mustard seed." And He will give you the world.

As long as I'm passing the hat, have another parable:

The two senators—one a Democrat and the other a Republican—had been fighting for years. Finally, a mutual friend insisted they have a drink together and bury the hatchet —but not in each other. Raising his glass the Democrat said: "Here's wishing you what you're wishing me."

"Oh," yelled the Republican, "now you're starting in again!"

"The Kingdom of God is within you." It took me a long time to realize that truth. My uncle came from his vacation one summer and told me, "There are thirty-eight guys in my office that I have to straighten out when I go back to work." That's when I realized that it's my uncle that has to change—they couldn't be all out of step but him. That's when I knew that it is I that must make my own world.

I make a lot of trips to Asia as well as Europe and I decided a long time ago that the Parisians were the worst hosts in the world. All cabdrivers in Paris were nasty, the waiters were arrogant, the customs men grouchy, and the people in general were impatient and hostile and hated Americans as well as themselves and their jobs. I found them all impossible to deal with.

When my uncle told me about the thirty-eight guys he had to straighten out, I remembered Thackeray's words. "The world is a looking glass—and gives back to every man the reflection of his own face." The next time I went to Paris I remembered this had to be the result of my own thinking and outlook. To paraphrase my old friend Martin Luther King, Jr., as soon as I got off the plane, "I smiled the hell out of them" —and you know something? I didn't find one unhappy room clerk, cabdriver, waiter or policeman. Even the customs men were pleasant.

Try it—you'll like it—and so will everybody you do business with—your partner, your neighbor, the bus driver—even your mother-in-law. The fastest way to correct the other guy's attitude is to correct your own.

And before you can say Archie Bunker, "The wolf also shall dwell with the lamb . . . and the leopard shall lie down with the kid . . . and the calf and the young lion and fatling together; and a little child shall lead them." (Isaiah 11:6)